MIDDLE EAST
MISSION

MIDDLE EAST MISSION

The Story of a Major Bid for
Peace in the Time of Nasser
and Ben-Gurion

Elmore Jackson

W · W · NORTON & COMPANY · NEW YORK · LONDON

Library of Congress Cataloging in Publication Data
Jackson, Elmore, 1910—
Middle East mission.
    Includes index.
1. Egypt—Foreign relations—Israel. 2. Israel—
Foreign relations—Egypt. 3. Jewish-Arab relations—
1949–1967. 4. Jackson, Elmore, 1910–   . 5. Society of
Friends—Biography. I. Title.
DT82.5.I7J33 1983   327.6205694   83-6299

ISBN 0-393-01785-0

W. W. Norton & Company, Inc., 500 Fifth Avenue, New York, N. Y. 10110
W. W. Norton & Company Ltd., 37 Great Russell Street, London WC1B 3NU
1 2 3 4 5 6 7 8 9 0

Contents

Preface

IN THE LATE spring and summer of 1955, before Prime Minister Gamal Abdel Nasser of Egypt made his dramatic turn to Eastern Europe for arms supply, he made a major effort to get a political settlement with Israel.

It may come as a surprise to the international community that Nasser—the vigorous apostle of Arab nationalism—should have taken such an initiative. Had it succeeded, the British-French-Israeli attack on Suez in 1956, and three subsequent Middle Eastern wars, including the recent one bringing such devastation to Lebanon, might not have taken place. Many years of recrimination and bloodshed might have been avoided.

By informal agreement at the time, the full story of these negotiations has never been told. Arab-Israeli tensions were running high, and any Arab leader who entered into negotiations with Israel could expect charges from Arab colleagues that he was selling out the Palestinian cause. So confidentiality was agreed upon—to be abrogated only if the negotiations produced prompt and dramatic results, or if later events should make its continuance politically unnecessary.

With such charismatic national leaders as David Ben-Gurion and Prime Minister Nasser having been intimately involved in negotiations which, had they succeeded, could have forestalled Egypt's Eastern European arms accord, it is perhaps surprising that confidentiality has been maintained for so long. If the silence was to be broken, however, it was appropriate for the first public reference to have been in Moshe Sharett's diaries, recently published in Hebrew. Sharett was Israeli Prime Minister at the time, having taken over the position from Ben-Gurion when the latter retired to the Negev. Ben-Gurion, the preeminent political figure, was now back in the cabinet as Defense Minister, but no one worked harder than Sharett to bring the negotiations to a satisfactory conclusion.

Following the reference in Sharett's diaries, discussion began among those who had been directly involved in 1955 as to the appropriateness and timeliness of a full report being made.

It soon became apparent that such a report could have significant implications for the development of the present peace process in the Middle East.

It could be important to King Hussein for the Jordanian people, the larger Arab public, and the international community to know that the King's earlier efforts to get a settlement with Israel were supplemented by Nasser's own initiative.

It could be important for the leadership of the Palestine Liberation Organization, who on occasion has expressed the view that President Nasser would never have done what President Anwar el-Sadat did, to know that Nasser indeed did initiate a serious negotiation looking toward an overall settlement.

It could be important to President Hosni Mubarak for the Egyptian people and the international community to know that President Sadat was not the first or the only Egyptian leader to have taken an initiative for a peace settlement with Israel—that Sadat was preceded in his effort by his principal revolutionary colleague, Gamal Abdel Nasser.

And lastly, it could be important to Prime Minister Menachim Begin and the Israeli people to know that there may, in fact, have been more continuity in Egyptian policy over the last three decades than had previously been assumed.

Thus a report that was originally projected as an important footnote to history may become an aid to the current peace process.

This is the story of the negotiations by the one who was asked to conduct them. While I was at the time familiar in general with Middle Eastern questions, and had assisted in formulating United Nations plans for the administration of international assistance for Palestine refugees as Arab-Jewish hostilities flared following partition, I could by no means have been considered a Middle East expert. I had, however, come to know many officials in both Israel and Egypt and had many personal friends among them.

The first two chapters of the following report describe the circumstances that led to my taking on, at the urging of Quaker colleagues and of senior officials in Jerusalem, Cairo, and the United States government, a formidable assignment. Suffice it to say here that I am not certain I would have had the courage to assume it had I not had experience for several months as a member of a United Nations mission attempting to bring Prime Minister Jawaharlal Nehru and Prime Minister Khwaji Nazimuddin to an agreement in the then bitter dispute between India and Pakistan over the princely state of Kashmir. The issues, of course, were strikingly different. But the respective personal chemistries bore some resemblance.

As I began work on the report I found the handwritten notes I had made, following meetings with Nasser, Ben-Gurion, and Sharett, both more complete and more legible than I had anticipated. The memories of the other participants who are still living have been very helpful. Perhaps not surprisingly, I found that the story of the negotiations fit, like the last few pieces of a picture puzzle, into the oddly shaped vacant spaces left—in this case—by Middle Eastern historians.

Many people, thus, have assisted in the preparation of this report. Ambassador Nabil Elaraby, formerly Deputy Permanent Representative to the United Nations and now the Egyptian Ambassador to India, took a special interest, discussed the matter with

Dr. Mahmoud Fawzi, former Foreign Minister and Premier, before the latter's death, and secured his endorsement for a report on the project in which he was so deeply involved. Dr. Ahmed Hussein, who, as the Egyptian Ambassador in Washington, had been a principal aid in the initiative, was most generous in the time spent in reviewing and discussing a draft of the report when I was in Cairo in June 1982, as was Mahmoud Riad, formerly Egyptian Ambassador to Syria and Secretary-General of the Arab League, and subsequently Egyptian Foreign Minister.

Gideon Rafael, formerly a principal assistant to Prime Minister Sharett and subsequently Ambassador to the United Nations and to the United Kingdom—the quarterback of the negotiations on the Israeli side—has been most helpful and has reviewed and commented on two drafts of the report, as has Meado Zaki, my colleague at the time.

I am much indebted to those listed above and to many official and unofficial persons deeply concerned with Middle Eastern affairs for very helpful discussions of Egyptian-Israeli relations, in 1955 and since. None of them, however, should be held responsible for omissions or commissions in this report.

Some of the most productive writing was done while Elisabeth Jackson and I were guests of the Rockefeller Foundation at the Villa Serbelloni in Bellagio, Italy, during the summer of 1982. Working in that unique location is a privilege for which the Foundation deserves profuse thanks.

I could not have asked for more perceptive and congenial publishing and editorial assistance than that provided by Donald S. Lamm and Mary Cunnane of W. W. Norton. From the beginning they have seen the importance of the story being told of this early effort in shuttle diplomacy at a major crossroads in Middle Eastern history. I am also grateful to Margaret Hope Bacon and Paul Brink of the American Friends Service Committee for their encouragement and assistance. Anyone having anything to do with United Nations documents is fortunate, as I was, to have the interest and effective assistance of Jack Belwood of the UN Archives. And lastly, I must emphasize that this project would never have been accomplished without the unstinting assistance of Elisabeth Jackson and Karen Kreller. The former has known, instinctively, when I needed companionship and when I did not. The latter has typed innumerable drafts, straightened out sentences, and provided a logistic support for which I will always be deeply grateful.

March 1983
Newtown, Pennsylvania

MIDDLE EAST
MISSION

I.

The Years of Prelude

PRESIDENT ANWAR EL-SADAT'S dramatic trip to Jerusalem in November 1977 was not the first Egyptian effort to bring peace between Israel and her Arab neighbors. In the spring of 1955, several months before Prime Minister Nasser shocked the West—and even many of his Arab friends—by turning to Eastern Europe for massive arms supply, he initiated a major effort for a settlement with Israel.

The channel he chose was an unexpected one. American Quakers, well known to the Egyptians and the Israelis through their humanitarian work in the Middle East, and especially for their administration of international aid to the Palestine refugees in the Gaza Strip in 1949 and 1950, were approached by senior Egyptian officials with—it subsequently became clear—Prime Minister Nasser's complete support, to see if they would be willing to explore the possibility of a political settlement between Egypt and Israel. Nasser was under heavy pressure from his generals for a major new arms supply. He feared his arms negotiations with the United States were going nowhere. If he could get a basic settlement with Israel—or at least some acceptable modus vivendi—Egypt's security situation would be very much less acute and he could avoid having to turn to what he considered to be his last major option—an arms agreement with Eastern Europe. He knew that to be a course fraught with political hazards and military uncertainties.

While the Egyptian approach came as a complete surprise to the Quakers, they were not without background for the exploration.

Nasser's initial experience with Quakers had been in 1949, in the early weeks of Quaker administration of the Palestine refugee relief program in the Gaza Strip. Indeed, the manner in which the Egyptian peace initiative unfolded owes much to this 1949 contact. But Quaker educational and humanitarian work in the Middle East had begun some seventy years earlier with the establishment by American Quakers of a school for girls in Ramallah, on the West Bank of the Jordan River, some ten miles northeast of Jerusalem. British Quakers for almost as long a period had conducted a school at Brummana, in the foothills of the Lebanon range east of Beirut. Subsequently a school for boys was established in Ramallah. The schools drew students from other areas of the Arab Middle East, and many graduates became leaders in the countries from which they came.

During World War II the American Friends Service Committee, headquartered in Philadelphia and the largest of the Quaker service agencies, became deeply involved in the resettlement in the United States of Jewish refugees from Hitler's Germany. It was a program that brought the Committee into close touch with American Jewish leadership.

With the creation of the United Nations in 1945 and the expectation that, with the British desirous of relinquishing their Mandate over Palestine, the new organization would be forced to make fundamental decisions about the future of the area, it was only natural that Quaker concerns for both Arabs and Jews should come to center in part on anticipated United Nations action. Indeed there were many areas in which Quaker wartime activity was related to programs being undertaken by the new organization. The American Friends Service Committee thus decided to establish, in cooperation with British Quakers, a liaison office at the United Nations, with an agenda that included a large number of issues before the UN with which Quakers had both considerable experience and a continuing concern. In the fall of 1948, I left my position as Assistant Executive Secretary of the Committee to become Director of this new program in New York.

In November 1947 the United Nations General Assembly had adopted a partition plan for Palestine.* As the time approached for the end of the British Mandate—May 14, 1948—there had been an increase of violence between the Arab and Jewish communities. With the proclamation of the State of Israel there was an escalation of hostilities as Egypt, Jordan, and Syria, supported by other Arab states, launched attacks against the new state.

It was a situation that quickly led to thousands of Arabs fleeing into areas allocated to Arab Palestine under the UN Partition Plan, and into other areas controlled by the Arab armies. There was a large influx of refugees, something over 200,000, into the Gaza Strip, a narrow band of land about five miles wide, extending along the Mediterranean coast for some twenty-two miles northward from the Sinai border.

At the urging of relief agencies in the Jerusalem area, Quakers had provided some funds for medical aid to refugees. The new Israeli government had also indicated that it would welcome discussions about the possibility of a Quaker team coming to Israel to assist in refugee settlement. Subsequent negotiations led to a relief and welfare program with refugees in western Galilee, and then with Arabs in the old walled city of Acre, a few miles north of Haifa—a program that continued over several years.

But Quaker leadership in Philadelphia, deeply concerned with the mounting violence in the area, had already been drawn into discussions of how it could be restrained. As early as February 1948, Clarence Pickett, the energetic and gifted Executive Secretary of the American Friends Service Committee, and Rufus Jones, professor of philosophy at Haverford College, the Committee's distinguished chairman, had been approached with the suggestion that Quakers take the initiative in organizing an appeal by Christian, Jewish, and Moslem leadership for a cessation of hostilities in

*See map of UN Partition Plan, page 20.

UN PARTITION PLAN – 1947
AND
UN ARMISTICE LINES – 1949

—·—·— Boundary of Former Palestine Mandate

PLAN OF PARTITION, 1947

Arab State
Jewish State
Jerusalem

– – – Armistice Demarcation lines, 1949
(Shown where at variance with Mandate boundary.)

LEBANON

Tyre

Quneitra

SYRIA

GOLAN

Nahariyya

Acre

Haifa

Safad

Lake
Tiberias

Nawa

Shef ar'am

Tiberias

Nazareth

Hadera

Jenin

Jordan

Netanya

Tulkarm

Kefar Sava

Qalqilya

Nablus

Tel Aviv

Arab
Jaffa

WEST

BANK

Rishon Le Zion

Ramle

Ramallah

Amman

Rehovot

Jericho

Latrun

Jerusalem

MEDITERRANEAN

Bethlehem

SEA

Hebron

Gaza

Dead

GAZA

Sea

JORDAN

Khan Yunis

Rafah

Beersheba

El Arish

ISRAEL

SINAI

EGYPT

0   10   20   30km
0   10   20   30mi

The designations employed and the presentation of
material on this map do not imply the expression of
any opinion whatsoever on the part of the Secretariat
of the United Nations concerning the legal status of
any country, territory, city or area or of its authorities, or
concerning the delimitation of its frontiers or boundaries.

Elat

Gulf of
Aqaba

LEBANON

ISRAEL

SYRIA

Tel Aviv

Jerusalem

JORDAN

EGYPT

0   30km
0   30mi

MAP NO. 3067   UNITED NATIONS
SEPTEMBER 1979

Jerusalem, a city sacred to all three great religions. After consultation with a number of interested religious leaders an appeal was
dispatched to Rabbi Isaac Hertzog, chief rabbi of Jerusalem, and
to Amin Bey Abdulhabi of the Supreme Moslem Council in Jerusalem.

No responses to the appeal had been received by Easter Sunday,
March 28, so the text was released to the press. The following day
an endorsement came from Rabbi Hertzog. Believing that the appeal should be supplemented with personal approaches, British and
American Quakers sent two of their more experienced members—
James Vail, a chemical engineer with extensive international experience, from Philadelphia, and Edgar Castle, a successful educational administrator from London—to Jerusalem for direct discussions. On April 28 Quaker leaders in Philadelphia and London
were informed that the Secretary of the Arab League had advised
the two visiting Quakers that the League was announcing its spon-
sorship of the truce for the Old City of Jerusalem and the Mount
of Olives.

With a ceasefire for Jerusalem becoming effective early in May
1948, British and American Quakers had the satisfaction of know-
ing that their initiative had played some part in the successful
negotiations.

The work on behalf of this initial truce probably set the stage for
another development. With the British relinquishing responsibility
for government functions under the Mandate, the United Nations
had developed a plan for a temporary UN administration of Jerusalem. On May 7, Andrew Cordier, Executive Assistant to UN Secretary-General Trygve Lie, telephoned Clarence Pickett to say that
Jewish and Arab leaders had united in approving Mr. Pickett as
municipal commissioner for Jerusalem. His role was not defined as
primarily administrative but rather as one in which he would keep
in close touch with both Arabs and Jews and attempt to see that
the joint administration of Jerusalem became a working reality.

Clarence Pickett, however, was not certain that he should leave
his important post in Philadelphia to take up the work in Jerusalem, and so Harold Evans, a leading Philadelphia lawyer active in
American Friends Service Committee affairs, was persuaded to

take on the assignment instead. He was approved as a substitute by the Arab and Jewish leaders. James Vail, who had participated in the discussions, held in the Middle East, on the initial Jerusalem truce, agreed to return to the area with him. Shortly after they arrived in Cairo, enroute to Jerusalem, they were informed that the Egyptian government no longer supported the idea of a UN municipal commissioner for Jerusalem. In the meantime fighting had escalated, with much of it centering in the Jerusalem area. Count Folke Bernadotte of Sweden was appointed UN Mediator. Since it was not possible for the office of municipal commissioner to develop as planned, Bernadotte invited Harold Evans and James Vail to come to Jerusalem and associate themselves with his efforts. The fact that Harold Evans had been approved by both Jewish and Arab leaders for a delicate though different task added a positive element in a tense situation. After Bernadotte's assassination by Jewish terrorists in September, the UN mediation effort continued under the skillful direction of Ralph Bunche, who was appointed Acting Mediator. The two Quakers then returned to Philadelphia.

It was against this background that the American Friends Service Committee was approached by the United Nations in October 1948 to see if it would be willing to assist in administering a program of international aid to the approximately eight hundred thousand Arab refugees from territory either allotted to Israel in the UN partition resolution or controlled by Israeli military forces. Quaker international work had become somewhat better known a few months earlier when the Committee, together with its British counterpart organization, the Friends Service Council, had received the 1947 Nobel Peace Prize.*

When the query was received in Philadelphia from the UN Secretary-General's office about Quaker participation in the Palestine relief program, I was in London on my way to the UN General Assembly meetings then being held in Paris. Speeding up my arrival in Paris, I joined UN and Red Cross officials in drawing up

---

*See Appendix I for statement by Gunnar Jahn, chairman of the Nobel Committee and Director of the Bank of Norway, at the presentation ceremony in Oslo, December 10, 1947.

the plans under which the League of Red Cross Societies took responsibility for administering the program of international aid to Palestine refugees in Lebanon, Syria, and Jordan, the International Committee of the Red Cross assumed responsibility in Israel, in other Israeli-controlled areas, and in Jordan-occupied areas of the West Bank, and the American Friends Service Committee took responsibility in the Egyptian-occupied Gaza area, with a degree of participation in Israel by arrangement between the agencies.

As the negotiations neared agreement we were joined by Stanton Griffis, an enterprising and attractive U.S. moviemaker, and former Ambassador to Egypt, who had been appointed by Trygve Lie to be Director of the United Nations Relief for Palestine Refugees, the supervisory body established by the UN General Assembly to coordinate policy and receive funds for administration by the three private agencies. We were also joined by Colin Bell, of the Foreign Service Section of the American Friends Service Committee, a veteran relief worker who had headed the Friends Ambulance Unit in China. The two men arrived in Paris on the same plane: Stanton Griffis in first-class Pullman accommodations, Colin Bell in economy class.

The initial UN plan called for a nine-month emergency program at a cost of $32,000,000. Subsequently the United Nations was to spend billions in caring for the refugees, with much of the funding coming from the United States.

Egyptian forces were in control in Gaza, and it was understood that Quaker willingness to administer the program in that area was dependent on Egyptian approval. Dr. Mahmoud Fawzi, Egyptian Foreign Minister, in Paris for the 1948 UN General Assembly, quickly gave that assent. As the former Egyptian Consul-General in Jerusalem he was intimately familiar with Palestine affairs.

Since the American Friends Service Committee was already working with refugees in Israel, the UN invitation and the Egyptian response were explained to Ambassador Abba Eban, then a member of the Israeli General Assembly Delegation and later to become Israel's Foreign Minister. It was emphasized that Quakers might initially need Israeli cooperation in getting supplies into Gaza. He pledged that cooperation, and, indeed, general Israeli assistance was soon enlisted, although in a somewhat different manner than had been anticipated.

During the early weeks of the Gaza operation a unit of about three thousand Egyptian troops remained encircled by Israeli forces at Faluja in the Negev, not far from the Gaza Strip. Gamal Abdel Nasser, then a colonel in the Egyptian army, was serving as Chief of Staff to Said Taha, an Egyptian brigade commander in the enclave. With the encouragement of the United Nations, Quakers negotiated agreements with the Israelis and with the Egyptian army that permitted food supplies to be taken through the Israeli and Egyptian lines to the local civilian population in the enclave, which, like the Egyptian forces, were cut off from all outside sources of food supply. Colonel Nasser handled the negotiations on behalf of the Egyptian army and carried out the subsequent distribution to the complete satisfaction of the Quaker group. There were no complaints—nor was there any suspicion—of diversion of supplies. A relationship of confidence developed that led to several long evenings in which Colonel Nasser and the Quaker convoy team sat around darkening campfires discussing the differences and similarities between Quaker and Islamic thought, especially in the field of social ethics—those areas in which religious tenets, personal philosophy, and the need for social and political action intersect. Nasser's philosophical interest was later reflected in his book *Egypt's Liberation: The Philosophy of the Revolution.* *

At the time of the Egyptian-Israeli armistice Nasser's unit at Faluja was permitted to retire to Egypt with full military honors. Much of Nasser's subsequent prestige in Egypt was due to the fact that his was the principal Egyptian front-line unit in the Palestine conflict which had not been forced to retreat or surrender.

These relationships between the Quakers and Colonel Nasser and other Egyptian and Israeli officials, largely as a result of the relief operation in Gaza, led to a continuing confidence over the succeeding years. Throughout the sixteen months in which Quakers administered the Gaza program before turning the administration over to the United Nations, they maintained the unit in Israel,

*Public Affairs Press, Washington, D.C., 1955.

working first with Arab refugees and then with the Arab population in Acre. Later they undertook rural development work in Jordan.

But it was the Gaza relief operation—and especially the relationship of confidence that developed with Nasser at Faluja—which set the stage for the Egyptian approach to Quakers in the spring of 1955.

II

The Egyptian Proposal

DURING THE EARLY 1950s Quakers were frequently encouraged by Israeli officials to try, on the basis of this background, to bring about some informal understanding or modus vivendi between Israel and Egypt. The suggestions were made at various times by members of the Israeli delegation at the UN or by officials of the Israeli Ministry of Foreign Affairs who had come to the UN General Assembly. Quakers had been slow to respond to these overtures on the grounds that without a clear opening for mediatory activity, we felt we should stick to our humanitarian work.

In April 1955, however, Dr. Ahmed Hussein, the Egyptian Ambassador in Washington and a personal friend of Prime Minister Nasser's,* got in touch with Quakers to say he felt the time had come to see if something could be worked out. Ambassador Hussein had started his public career in the Egyptian government's agricultural extension service, eventually heading that program. Subsequently he had served as Minister of Social Affairs in the prerevolutionary Wafd government. Nasser had tried to persuade

*Colonel Nasser was made Prime Minister in March 1954 and elected President in June 1956.

him to take a similar position after the revolution, but Dr. Hussein
had declined. He finally agreed to become ambassador in Washington for a year or two with the understanding that he would report
not to Dr. Fawzi, the Foreign Minister, but directly to Nasser. He
was to remain in the position for five years. Aziza Hussein, the
Ambassador's wife, had already entered on what was to become an
important career in Egyptian—and, ultimately, international—social welfare work.

Through his close friend Meado Zaki, Ambassador Hussein now
suggested a meeting with Quaker leaders to discuss the developing
situation in the Middle East. Meado was living in the United States
but had formerly been Dean of the Cairo School of Social Work
and Executive Secretary of the Egyptian Association of Social
Studies. He was well known to American Quaker leaders and had
been helpful in discussions with Egyptian officials when Harold
Evans and James Vail were in Cairo in 1948 enroute to Jerusalem;
later, during the period of Quaker administration of the refugee
relief program in Gaza, he had played an important role in developing the educational program in the camps. Arrangements were
made for Clarence Pickett, now retired as Executive Secretary of
the American Friends Service Committee, and Delbert Replogle,
a Quaker businessman from New Jersey, who, in the best Quaker
tradition of volunteer service, had taken several months off from
his business in 1949 to head the relief program in Gaza, to join
Ambassador and Mrs. Hussein and Meado Zaki for dinner at the
Egyptian Embassy in Washington on April 12. Delbert Replogle
was one of those who had become acquainted with then Colonel
Nasser during the Gaza relief operation.

In opening the discussion the Ambassador spoke of the persist-
ent difficulties in the Middle East and of his appreciation for the
continuing interest of Quakers. He spoke freely, suggesting that he
was giving his own opinion and not necessarily that of his government. He said he knew that any negotiations between Israel and
the Arabs would have to be carried on directly, but he felt Quakers
might be useful in bringing forward a suggested formula which, if
agreed to by Israel, would be of great interest to representatives of
the Arab states. He indicated that it was difficult for Egypt to take

any formal initiative in peace negotiations. It was easier for it to respond to suggestions made by others. It could then take some lead with the other Arab states. He emphasized the importance of Quakers early in any negotiations getting some positive gesture from the Israelis indicating their interest in moving toward a settlement.

On the refugee question, he felt there were two principal possibilities. A small number of refugees might return to Israel under a plan for the reuniting of families. Others might, in agreement with Israel, be settled in some part of the territory now occupied or claimed by Israel. He felt that the boundaries of the state of Israel as proposed by the UN should be restored.* He believed progress must and could be made on border questions and on refugee compensation. He did not think the internationalization of Jerusalem, as proposed by the United Nations, was important. Ambassador Hussein suggested that the U.S. State Department's position was that the time was not ripe for negotiation. But he himself felt that if an imaginative formula could be produced, that itself might create the timing for action. He indicated that, at the suggestion of Henry Byroade, the recently appointed U.S. Ambassador to Egypt, he had discussed a number of these ideas with Jacob Blaustein, an influential American Jewish leader who was close to the Israeli leadership. Mr. Blaustein was not one to be daunted by the difficulties and complexities of the Israeli-Arab conflict and had encouraged him to believe something along these lines might be worked out. He had formerly been President of the American Jewish Committee and he was at the time a principal stockholder in the American Oil Company, a company later absorbed into Standard Oil of Indiana. The Ambassador suggested Quakers talk with Mr. Blaustein and with George V. Allen, Assistant Secretary of State for Near Eastern, South Asian, and African Affairs.

The discussion with Ambassador Hussein had been candid, and while his proposal was an imposing one for Quakers to consider, it drew sufficiently on existing Quaker concerns and relationships

*See map of UN Partition Plan, p. 20.

in the Middle East so that those who joined in the Washington meeting, along with their colleagues in Philadelphia and New York, believed it must be taken seriously. The degree to which Ambassador Hussein was operating on his own and the extent to which the Egyptian government—and in particular Prime Minister Nasser—was a party to the initiative was at this point unclear.* But the Ambassador's general rationale was sufficiently persuasive that we decided to proceed with consultations with Assistant Secretary Allen and with Mr. Blaustein.

Mr. Pickett and Lewis Hoskins, his successor as Executive Secretary of the American Friends Service Committee, both had other heavy commitments, so it now fell to me to take the lead in arranging consultations and coordinating the Quaker response.

George Allen thought the exploration should clearly proceed. He believed it significant that Ambassador Hussein had taken the initiative for the meeting. The advisability of trying for a general settlement between Israel and Egypt was discussed. George Allen suggested that Quakers keep in mind the possibility of limited settlements of specific issues.

Mr. Allen informed us of the negotiations being conducted by Eric Johnston, a special envoy of President Eisenhower, on a plan for sharing the all too scarce water of the Jordan River. During three terms as President of the U.S. Chamber of Commerce, Mr. Johnston had been referred to as the first breath of fresh air to blow through the Chamber in twenty years. United States officials had persuaded him to interrupt what was to become a very successful eighteen-year stint as president of the Motion Picture Association of America to see if he could resolve the increasing conflict between the governments of Jordan, Syria, and Israel over the division of the limited flow of the Jordan River. Jordan wanted it for settlements in the Jordan Valley that could help resettle the Palestine refugees. Israel wanted to carry additional water to the Negev for

---

*In a discussion in Cairo on June 23, 1982, Ambassador Ahmed Hussein told me that from the beginning of his meetings with Quakers in April 1955 Nasser had supported the initiative, and that as the negotiations proceeded he had kept the Prime Minister fully informed.

new settlements for Jewish immigrants. The United States, believing that the experience of the Tennessee Valley Authority in developing a regional plan for water use might have some relevance to the use of the Jordan waters, had sent Gordon Clapp, chairman of the TVA, on a survey mission to the area. On the strength of his analysis, Eric Johnston had been asked to develop and seek agreement on a detailed plan. Mr. Allen believed the negotiations had a fifty-fifty chance of success.

Following this meeting the Quaker group decided to focus initially, in any discussions that might take place, on a few limited issues, but to remain flexible if the way opened for wider discussions.

Consultations were then held with two experienced officials at the United Nations, both of whom were familiar with Quaker work in the Middle East: Andrew Cordier, still Executive Assistant to the Secretary-General—now Dag Hammarskjold—and James Barco, Counselor and principal political adviser on the Middle East at the United States Mission to the United Nations. Both officials encouraged us to proceed with the exploration.

A meeting followed with Jacob Blaustein. He indicated that he was involved in some informal discussions on the Middle East and would know soon whether they were likely to bear fruit. He thought if Quakers moved ahead with the inquiry there might be some advantages in working together. He said he had been largely responsible several years previously for the Israeli offer to take back 100,000 refugees—an offer made by the Israelis in connection with the negotiations being conducted by the UN's Palestine Conciliation Commission. At the time the Arab states did not consider the number being proposed for return to be sufficiently large. The UN Commission had been charged by the General Assembly with the responsibility of effecting an overall settlement of the Palestine problem, and resolution of the refugee question was only one aspect of its mandate. It had never been able, however, to make any progress in resolving the principal issues in conflict.

It was agreed with Mr. Blaustein that we would keep in touch.

At about this time, Ambassador Hussein informed me that Egyptian Foreign Minister Mahmoud Fawzi would be coming to the United States in mid-July for the UN Tenth Anniversary meeting in San Francisco. The Ambassador suggested that this would provide an excellent opportunity for us to discuss the proposed exploration with a senior Egyptian official. We had had extensive contact with Dr. Fawzi during the Gaza relief operation and knew him to be a very perceptive man with balanced judgment. Despite the delay that it would cause, it was decided to wait until after the meeting with Dr. Fawzi to discuss the possible inquiry with the Israelis. In view of the importance of the general exploration, we felt we needed to know how the Foreign Minister saw it, and how he felt it could best be conducted.

Four of us met with Dr. Fawzi in his suite at the Ambassador Hotel in New York on July 15. Lewis Hoskins, Colin Bell, who had participated in the Gaza relief negotiations in Paris in 1948, and Sydney Bailey, a British Quaker associate in the Quaker program at the United Nations, joined me in the meeting.

It was clear from the beginning of our discussion that the Foreign Minister had been a full partner in proposing the course of action suggested by Ambassador Hussein. He said he would welcome a Quaker effort to find a "solution" and emphasized the importance of a solution being found promptly. He said, referring to the Middle East, "the apple is spoiling and will get worse." He said the Arabs would rather wait than give in on two counts: (1) some repatriation of refugees and compensation of those choosing not to return, and (2) territorial adjustments that would link the Arab communities (presumably across the Negev). He indicated the Egyptians were not interested in any new territory—not even the Gaza Strip. Any territorial concessions by Israel should be to one of the other Arab states. Egypt would prefer that any refugee compensation come from Israel, but he said the source did not matter too much. Compensation should be adequate to cover the permanent settlement of the refugees.

Dr. Fawzi emphasized that the need now was for "an imaginative, courageous approach." He stressed the importance of an over-all settlement and expressed doubts about the utility of a step-by-step approach. At one point he implied that the time might come when "others" might have to say to the conflicting parties that "this must end." The Foreign Minister did not suggest who these others might be, but the implication was that it might have to be the Great Powers. He was asked whether he thought a Quaker inquiry should involve discussions in the Middle East or whether they should be carried on elsewhere. His initial reaction was reserved, but as the discussion proceeded he became emphatic that Quakers should follow the exploration wherever it led—including a visit to the area if that seemed indicated. We asked if the fact that the inquiry would be conducted by Americans would be a handicap. He said, "No—it would be an asset."

The meeting with the Foreign Minister settled two basic questions. First, it was clear that Ambassador Hussein's initiative was strongly supported in Cairo, and second, the Egyptian officials believed the Middle Eastern situation was deteriorating and called for a major effort to find the basis for a general settlement. Dr. Fawzi's comments carried a sense of urgency. At the time we did not know how critical the situation had already become—or how high the stakes would ultimately become in the ensuing two months.

But the time was now clearly at hand to talk with the Israelis. I called Ambassador Reginald Kidron, the Israeli Ambassador at the United Nations, and we met promptly. After I had informed him of the Egyptian proposal, he said he would brief his colleagues and was certain his government would be interested in cooperating. Arrangements were made for me to see Abba Eban, the Israeli Ambassador in Washington. Discussions within the Quaker community now came to a head, and, subject to further discussions with Ambassadors Eban and Hussein, it was agreed the exploration should go forward. It was suggested that I take on the assignment and leave during the last week in July for several weeks of shuttling between Jerusalem and Cairo. Shuttle diplomacy was uncommon in those days, and all things considered, it was a formidable prospect. I had on two occasions served as a member of the United Nations mission attempting to mediate the Kashmir dispute between India and Pakistan. But being a member of a team is very different from being on this kind of individual assignment.

Further discussions were held with Andrew Cordier at the UN,

James Barco at the U.S. Mission, and Jacob Blaustein. The latter offered his full cooperation and, in particular, offered to join me for discussions in Israel if at any time I thought that would be useful.

Abba Eban had been well briefed by Ambassador Kidron. He said he was certain anything we could do would be welcomed. A visit to the Middle East would be a good thing, he thought, the only question being that of timing. He knew Eric Johnston had hoped for a clear field for his Jordan water negotiations, and he believed Johnston might be near to an agreement. He was having lunch with him that day and would, following that, have a judgment on those negotiations, although he thought the Department of State would have the best judgment on timing. Ambassador Eban said he would consult with Prime Minister Moshe Sharett over the weekend about the proposed mission and about the timing of a visit. He suggested I telephone him on the following Tuesday.

In a meeting later in the day, George Allen said he thought we should proceed, recognizing that other approaches were also being made. He did not think the mission would interfere in any way with Eric Johnston's activities. He mentioned a recent visit to the Middle East by Ira Hirshman, a prominent American Jewish leader, in which Mr. Hirshman had had discussions in both Jerusalem and Cairo, but with inconclusive results—perhaps in part because on his second (and last) trip to Cairo Prime Minister Nasser was ill.

On Tuesday Ambassador Eban reported that his government welcomed the exploration and would be glad to cooperate.

Ambassador Hussein was pleased to learn of the response from the Israelis and the Department of State. Once again he confirmed that we would have his government's full cooperation. He said he was leaving on July 30 for Cairo and would be available there to help arrange interviews. He was now very clear that the discussions should be held in the Middle East. While I was in the area he thought it would be useful for me to talk with Mahmoud Riad, the Egyptian ambassador to Syria; he would write him in preparation. He believed Mr. Blaustein would be useful in discussions in Israel and that it would be helpful also to have Meado Zaki with us in Cairo. He said I should inform Dr. Fawzi about my travel schedule just as soon as it became definite.

Before we parted Ambassador Hussein sketched in what he considered to be some of the basic elements of a settlement. He did not think compensation for the refugees unwilling or unable to return was a major problem. Boundaries were the real difficulty. Some refugees must be settled in what was once "Palestine," in areas in which the Israelis had overrun the UN partition lines. Some should be settled in the Negev adjacent to Jordan in territory that could then be attached to Jordan. He said the resettled refugees need not come from Gaza. They could come from Jordan, where many refugees were still living in temporary quarters.

My Quaker colleagues had suggested that enroute to Israel, where the governmental discussions would begin, I should visit very briefly two Quaker development projects in Jordan. Quakers had also been encouraged to explore in both Jordan and Israel the possibilities of the Hadassah Hospital on Mount Scopus being reopened and administered by Quakers on a nonpolitical basis to meet medical needs both in Israel and in the West Bank of the Jordan. Because of its commanding position in East Jerusalem, Mount Scopus had been heavily fought over following the UN partition of Palestine. Any use involved sensitive political and security issues. Dr. George Perera, Associate Dean of Columbia Medical School in New York, was, on behalf of Quakers, studying the need and the feasibility of reopening the hospital, and I was scheduled to participate in those discussions.

On August 3 I left for London and Beirut, enroute to Amman and then Jerusalem. George Perera and I met in Beirut, had the planned discussions in Jordan, and headed for the American Colony Hotel in Arab East Jerusalem, where we were to spend our last night before crossing into Israel. On the morning of August 9, after clearing through the Jordanian checkpoint at the Mandelbaum Gate, we lugged our heavy bags across the hot and dusty no man's land that separated Arab and Jewish Jerusalem.

III

The Intensive Negotiations in Jerusalem and Cairo

I HAD GIVEN Ambassador Eban an estimate as to when Dr. Perera and I would reach Israel but because of the necessary discussions in Jordan had not been able to indicate the specific day. We were thus both surprised and pleased, as we reached the checkpoint on the Israeli side of the Mandelbaum Gate, to be met by an aide from the Israeli Foreign Ministry. He said he had been instructed to monitor the applications for entry and meet us on arrival. He escorted us to the King David Hotel and informed Gideon Rafael, an associate of Prime Minister Sharett, of our arrival.

One of our first appointments in Jerusalem was with E.L.M. Burns, the Canadian General who was chief of the United Nations Truce Supervision Organization (UNTSO), the international group responsible for ensuring compliance with the Armistice Agreements. Senior UN officials in New York had been concerned that I inform him in confidence of the general nature of the mission, and that Dr. Perera and I talk with him about the Hadassah Hospital proposal. He listened carefully to our explanations of the background on both inquiries. As a long-time realist who had seen many ideas for resolving Middle Eastern problems come and go, he was interested but reserved on the general exploration—despite its origin—and very cautious on the feasibility of the reopening of the Hadassah Hospital. He emphasized the sensitivity of the political and security issues surrounding Mount Scopus. We decided that Dr. Perera should continue his soundings, but fast-moving developments on the peace initiative prevented my being an active participant.

Gideon Rafael telephoned, and we met for dinner at the King David Hotel. Gideon had been a close associate of Moshe Sharett from the very beginning of the State of Israel. He had assisted Sharett in establishing the Foreign Ministry, and when David Ben-Gurion had taken leave from the Prime Ministership for a period of rest and reflection in the Negev, Gideon continued to work closely with Sharett, who took over as Prime Minister. We had become generally acquainted from his interest in the Quaker refugee relief work in Gaza and from his frequent trips to attend United Nations meetings in New York.

As could be expected, Gideon wanted to know in detail of the discussions with Egyptian officials. How serious were they? What was the extent of Nasser's personal interest? Were some measures to create confidence necessary before getting into the hard issues of boundaries and refugee resettlement? Would not these difficult questions have to be negotiated face-to-face? I gave him our judgment that the Egyptian officials were indeed serious, but not yet prepared for face-to-face negotiations. I told him of our impression that there was not time for special confidence-building measures. Confidence could arise from forward moves on key substantive issues. The Egyptians had emphasized the need for some positive indication of flexibility on the Israeli side if serious negotiation was to get under way. I thought I would need such a gesture if the current interest in Cairo was to be turned into genuine forward movement.

The initial meeting with Rafael at the King David was followed by a long lunch at Rafael's home with Prime Minister Sharett, Rafael, Ambassador Arthur Lourie from the Foreign Ministry, and Mr. Eliav, an assistant to Rafael.

This was my first extended meeting with Sharett. A slight, urbane man with dark hair and an even darker mustache, he impressed me as being extremely knowledgeable, thoroughly familiar with Middle Eastern and international affairs, with an understanding of Arab interests and dilemmas, and eager to come to some mutually satisfactory agreement.

At the luncheon I had an early opportunity to tell of our experience with Nasser in the Negev in 1949. Sharett appeared to accept the assessment I had given Rafael as to the serious interest of the Egyptians in the present exploration, and promptly turned the discussion to substantive issues. He asked what the Egyptians were interested in. I told him: (1) some repatriation of refugees, (2) compensation of refugees unwilling or unable to return, and (3) boundary adjustments. He said there could be a reuniting of families—with a wide definition of "family"—and compensation for other refugees. On boundaries he said Israel would consider some adjustments—some territory elsewhere for Gaza. He said no Israeli government could give away access to the Gulf of Aqaba. He did not think any Egyptian government would be much interested in a strip of sand on the Israeli-Egyptian border in the Sinai. He said he would consider a triangular territorial adjustment that included Jordan.

Rafael and Sharett then mentioned several interim steps that they thought would improve the climate: (1) an exchange of prisoners, (2) a reduction of tension in the Gulf of Aqaba, (3) stopping incursions across armistice lines, and (4) a cessation of inflammatory speeches.

As we parted I emphasized that I was certain that flexibility on basic issues would be necessary if the discussions were to continue.

Rafael accompanied me to a meeting the following day with Mr. Ben-Gurion. The latter had in February returned to the cabinet as Minister of Defense. Short, stocky, with a shock of receding white hair and a lively mind and sense of humor, he was a patriarchal figure with a very appealing personality. While it was our first meeting, I had followed his career closely. He was at his philosophical and charismatic best. He asked about Quakers, how they were organized, and their beliefs. He talked of Buddhism and his recent talks with U Nu, former Prime Minister of Burma. I told him Quakers had been hesitant to undertake this exploratory mission. He said, "No. It is right for you to take it on."

I then explained that if it was to succeed I would need to leave Israel with something in hand. He liked this directness. He said Israel was prepared to live within existing borders, but there could be "no cession of territory." I asked if this meant no "adjustment of boundaries," and, in a qualification of his just-expressed assertion that there could be "no cession of territory," he mentioned several areas in which boundary adjustments could be considered. He confirmed that reuniting of families and refugee compensation were both possibilities. Our meeting closed with his saying he would go anywhere to talk to Prime Minister Nasser—even to Cairo. He said, "Nasser is a decent fellow who has the interest of his people genuinely at heart."

That evening Rafael and I had a concluding session with the Prime Minister at his home. Sharett expressed appreciation for the way in which the exploration was being conducted. He said he had been somewhat skeptical of the mission's success but felt the odds made it all the more important. He had seen U.S. Ambassador Edward Lawson a few days before and they had agreed it was the most promising of the various possibilities. He said we would not need to be concerned about implementation on the Israeli side. Either he or Mr. Ben-Gurion would be Prime Minister and would follow through on any agreements. If they had given their word they would deliver.

He wanted in closing to say a word about the raids launched from the Gaza Strip by Palestinian terrorists—or fedayeen, as they were called. He said Nasser must accept responsibility for what happened in the Gaza area. He felt Nasser was badly informed about what was going on. Israel, he said, had evidence that the armed intruders were centrally equipped.

It had been agreed that before I left Israel for Cairo, Rafael would take me on a brief trip to the Negev. It gave us the opportunity, between visits to a kibbutz and a close-up view of the armistice demarcation line separating the Israeli and Egyptian forces in the Gaza area, to talk more freely about substance and strategy. He confirmed Sharett's willingness to consider a triangular territorial and boundary settlement (Israel, Egypt, and Jordan). He said Ben-Gurion was prepared to be quoted on having said he would meet with Nasser and visit Cairo. Rafael emphasized that once discussions got started we would find Israel very flexible. "Surprisingly so," he said. I showed him my outline of the areas in which I thought they were prepared to consider concessions. He did not demur. He suggested that the talks begun in the Middle East might be continued at the fall UN General Assembly in New York, which he expected Sharett to attend.

At a final lunch with Rafael and Eliav in Jerusalem before leaving for Tel Aviv and Cairo, the two officials said they and their colleagues had been impressed by the opening round of discussions.

In Tel Aviv I saw Ambassador Lawson, giving him a rundown on the talks with Israeli leaders. He thought the talks in Jerusalem had gone very well and said he would notify the embassy in Cairo of my expected arrival the following day, August 18.

In 1955 there were, of course, no direct flights between Israel and Egypt. There were not even any closely connecting flights via Cyprus, Istanbul, or Athens. It was assumed no one would want to go from one country to the other on the same day. The usual route from Israel to Egypt was to fly to Cyprus, spend the night on this island off the Lebanese coast, then British-controled, and then the next day fly on to Cairo. It was the route I took.

Jerusalem had been a city set in rolling hills, aware of its place in history but bustling with modernization. Cairo was, of course, in great contrast. Set on a sandy plain bisected by the slow-moving Nile, modernization was proceeding but at a pace that reflected even deeper roots in history.

Meado Zaki was waiting for me at the Semiramis Hotel. We were soon closeted with Ambassador Hussein, and then with Foreign Minister Fawzi at his modest home near the pyramids. Meetings followed with Parker Hart, Deputy Chief of Mission at the U.S. Embassy, and with Henry Byroade. I had heard good things about Byroade from Ambassador Hussein but had not met him before. A West Point graduate, he had been made a brigadier general at age thirty-two because of a number of well-handled assignments—including in China and in connection with the Berlin blockade. At the age of thirty-eight he resigned his commission to become Assistant Secretary of State for Near Eastern, South Asian, and African Affairs. He had gotten on well with Nasser since arriving in Cairo as Ambassador on February 27, the day before an especially severe Israeli attack on Gaza.

The American and Egyptian officials were encouraged by the discussions in Israel. Dr. Fawzi and Ambassador Hussein thought Prime Minister Nasser would be interested and encouraged by the suggestions of the Israeli leaders on possible boundary adjustments, on refugee repatriation under a liberal interpretation of reuniting of families, on compensation for refugees unable or unwilling to return, and on the need and possibilities for a deescalation of recent cross-border violence. They arranged for me to meet with the Prime Minister.

The appointment was set for 7:45 on the evening of August 26 at the Revolutionary Command headquarters. The headquarters was located on an island in the Nile, across the main channel from the Semiramis Hotel. Dusk was settling in as Meado Zaki and I walked across the bridge. I had known enough about the Israeli leadership and their past approaches in the Middle East conflict to have some idea of what to expect in the discussions in Jerusalem. But despite some intensive briefing and research, I had little idea of what might emerge out of the discussions with Nasser. Meado and I lapsed into a thoughtful silence as we appraoched the gray stone headquarters building. We entered and the uniformed receptionist took our names, made a telephone call, and, after a brief conversation in Arabic, said that the Prime Minister would like to see me alone. Meado suggested he would wait and I was shown up a flight of stairs to the Prime Minister's quarters.

Nasser, a tall, youthful, broad-shouldered man, with an impressive athletic build and an engaging smile, was then in his thirty-seventh year. He was in informal army attire. He greeted me warmly, asking when I had arrived in Cairo and saying he understood I had had some interesting discussions in Israel. He referred to the cordial relationships he had had with the Quaker relief administrators in the Gaza area in 1949 at the time the Egyptian units were surrounded at Faluja in the Negev. He said that by the way they had handled the Gaza relief operation Quakers had won the respect and affection of the Egyptian people.

After a brief reference to present Quaker projects in Jordan and Israel our talk moved on to the discussions in Israel. He asked for my impressions. I reviewed the discussions with Sharett and Ben-Gurion in considerable detail. It was obvious that he had been a full party to the invitation to the Quakers to undertake the exploration and that he had been well briefed by Dr. Fawzi and Ambassador Hussein on my report of the discussions in Israel.

Nasser said that after Ben-Gurion took a leave from the Prime Ministership and Sharett took over he had developed a great deal of confidence in Sharett—so much so that he had agreed to informal Israeli-Egyptian exchanges, some of them in Paris.* But with Ben-Gurion's return to the Cabinet as Defense Minister, the Israeli attacks across the Gaza demarcation lines resumed. One particularly "vicious" attack on Gaza on February 28, he said, led him to break off the informal talks. Now he did not know whether he had confidence in either Sharett or Ben-Gurion. He said he had assured his people that Israel would cease the military attacks and urged that they overlook occasional incidents. But with the escalation of violence on the Israeli side he felt he now had no choice but to respond. His honor and that of his army was at stake. There had been another Israeli raid the preceding Thursday night.

I told the Prime Minister that I was going back to Israel on Sunday and asked if there was anything I could do to help restore confidence. He did not give a firm reply. I mentioned the Israeli suggestion of a prisoner exchange. He said he was not certain Israel held Egyptian prisoners comparable in importance to the Israeli prisoners held by the Egyptians. He would investigate and let me know on my next visit to Cairo. I reviewed the other Israeli suggestions for "climate improvement," but in none of them did he show as much interest as in a possible prisoner exchange.

Nasser was encouraged by the apparent Israeli flexibility on repatriation, compensation, and boundaries, and he pressed me for

*Gideon Rafael participated in some of these negotiations.

details. But he was also concerned with the recent escalation of cross-border violence. It was clear that a deescalation of violence would need to accompany substantive discussion if progress was to be made. So, pending discussions in Israel on the border violence, I turned the discussion to wider issues, saying I hoped there would be an improvement in Egyptian-U.S. relations. He said he would like that very much, but "equipment" was the important thing. He said deeds were what was needed. Speeches no longer impressed him. I suggested it would be an excellent thing if he could meet and talk with President Eisenhower. He said he admired the President and would very much welcome such an opportunity.

We had gotten on well. He was warm and cordial. I felt some trust had been established, but it was not at all clear that it could be translated into progress on any of the basic Arab-Israeli issues. It was clear, however, that he wanted to continue the discussion and that the expected me back in Cairo in a few days. My return, however, was to be sooner than either of us expected.

Dr. Fawzi had arranged for a young Air Force pilot to fly me to Gaza and back the next day. We flew in a single-engine plane that provided a panoramic view of the Suez area, then of El-Arish on the Mediterranean coast, and soon of the sand dunes, palm trees, orange groves, and stone houses of the Khan Yunis and Gaza areas—on which had been superimposed the tents and mud huts of approximately 200,000 Palestine refugees.

There had been few Quaker visitors to Gaza since our relief unit had turned operations over to the United Nations in 1950. I had expected it to be an unpublicized visit but found the mayor of Gaza had been informed. Ceremony came close to crowding out quiet fact finding. While it proved to be a long day, it was fascinating to see how so much humanity was managing to live with some dignity in so small a space. It was also interesting to see the Gaza Strip armistice demarcation line from the Israeli and Egyptian sides within such a short space of time.

The following morning I met with Ambassador Hussein and then with Ambassador Byroade, and in the afternoon flew to Cyprus. The two ambassadors thought the negotiations were still alive, but that the second round of discussions in Israel would be crucial. They were crucial, but in a somewhat different way than any of us had anticipated.

I arrived in Tel Aviv August 29 early in the afternoon. I had expected to take a taxi to Jerusalem. To my surprise I was met by an official from the Ministry of Foreign Affairs. He said he had instructions from Prime Minister Sharett to bring me directly to Ben-Gurion's home in Jerusalem. Ben-Gurion was in bed with a mild case of the flu but the two men would meet me there. I asked what was up. The escort said Sharett and Ben-Gurion would explain. When we arrived, three others were also present: Gideon Rafael; Jacob Hertzog, an assistant to Ben-Gurion; and Colonel Nehemia Argov, Ben-Gurion's military aide. As we sat around Ben-Gurion's bedside, Sharett and Ben-Gurion explained that there had been an increase of fedayeen attacks into Israel from the Gaza Strip over the preceding few days. In response, earlier that day they had authorized a large Israeli attack against Khan Yunis at the southern end of the Gaza Strip. They asked whether I could bring any reassuring news from the discussions in Cairo. If so, they might consider canceling the order for the attack.

I told them of the Cairo discussions, of the reasons for Nasser pulling out of the Paris talks, of his interest in their substantive proposals and a prisoner exchange but of his unwillingness to reenter direct negotiations as long as the large-scale Israeli attacks continued. I gave them my assessment, in which Ambassadors Hussein and Byroade had concurred, that the basic negotiation was still alive, but said I thought it might not be if the projected attack occurred. I had the impression Sharett agreed with me. Ben-Gurion was more noncommittal. They thanked me for my candor and for the efforts I was making, and an aide drove me to the King David Hotel.

Gideon Rafael came to the hotel in the late evening. He said that after I left the meeting they had decided to cancel the attack, and, to make certain the order would be carried out, Ben-Gurion had sent Colonel Argov to the Negev to personally deliver the order.

The next morning Rafael again met me at the hotel. He said the evening before, when Colonel Argov got to the Negev, he found that the first military units were already across the demarcation line and into the Gaza Strip. But the units were pulled back before any casualties occurred. He said the fedayeen raids were continuing, however, and he did not know how long they could withhold retaliatory response if the bloody fedayeen activity continued. The press was displaying grim and gory pictures, and public opinion was deeply aroused. The public pressure was heavy for military retaliation.

A day later on a trip to Tel Aviv to see Ambassador Lawson, I saw many signs of military movement. On the return to Jerusalem I talked with General Burns, UNTSO Chief of Staff, who was also attempting to prevent an escalation of hostilities. Following the cancellation of the Khan Yunis raid, the Egyptians had accepted Burns's call for a ceasefire. The Israelis had not given a definite answer but had asked General Burns to obtain assurances that the Egyptian government "is ready to give guarantees for immediate, complete and definitive cessation of all further hostile acts."*

Both Ambassador Lawson and General Burns were very apprehensive. Rafael and Eliav came to see me in the late afternoon at the hotel. I emphasized again that I believed arrangements could be worked out to deescalate the violence, but that I believed a major raid into the Strip would pretty well doom my current effort. Late that night I got a call from Rafael saying that Prime Minister Sharett wanted to see me at his home at 7:45 the next morning.

When Rafael picked me up for the breakfast meeting with Sharett he said that the previous evening they had launched a large-scale attack against Khan Yunis. He said the Prime Minister wanted me to make a quick trip to Cairo with a message for Nasser. When we met, Sharett explained. He said that with the escalating fedayeen violence they felt they could no longer refrain from retaliation. But they definitely wanted an end to the reciprocal violence. He believed Nasser was a man of integrity. But there "had been some misunderstandings." Sharett said "the cycle of violence must be broken." Would I be willing to fly to Cairo late that afternoon carrying a message to Nasser that the Israelis wanted an end to the

---

*Headquarters statement, UN Truce Supervision Organization, Jerusalem, Palestine, August 30, 1955.

violence? They would be prepared now to adhere completely to General Burns's call for a ceasefire. If it would be useful, either he or Ben-Gurion would be willing to meet Nasser at kilometer 95 (on the Gaza Strip demarcation line) to work out a general modus vivendi in support of the armistice agreement. I told him I would like a little time to think it over—I was not certain that, arriving from Israel so soon after a large-scale raid, I would necessarily be welcome. Sharett said he was sure I would have credibility, because Nasser would know that the Israelis had canceled the previously mounted raid after talking with me—since it was highly unusual for them to pull military units back once they had been launched. Sharett said Ben-Gurion would like to see me at one o'clock.

In the talk with Ben-Gurion I had the impression that while he had supported the decision to reinstate the raid, he joined in genuinely wanting an end to the escalating violence.* He also still seemed to see possibilities in my basic exploration. He suggested that perhaps he and Nasser could meet somewhere on the Gaza demarcation line or, indeed, in Cairo, to work out some form of reinforcement for the armistice agreement, or even to begin a process that might lead to a political settlement. He was eloquent about the advantages of a settlement. He hoped I would be willing to go to Cairo promptly and discuss these possibilities with Prime Minister Nasser.

Ambassador Lawson had come to Jerusalem and he strongly supported the need for prompt discussions with Nasser. He thought because of the initial cancellation of the Khan Yunis raid I would have credibility as a third party. He believed Ben-Gurion's interest in progress toward a settlement had been deeply stirred. He said he could arrange the special permissions required for me to recross into Jordan through the Mandelbaum Gate and fly to Cairo from the east Jerusalem airport on an Air Jordan flight at 4:15 P.M. I decided to go.

---

*It has since been reported that Moshe Dayan, the Israeli Chief of Staff, resigned over the cancellation of the raid. Ben-Gurion finally persuaded him to withdraw his resignation, but as a condition he was permitted to reinstate the raid two days later. Gideon Rafael, *Destination Peace: Three Decades of Israeli Foreign Policy.* (New York: Stein and Day, 1981, p. 43).

Parker Hart, U.S. Deputy Chief of Mission, met me at the Cairo airport. He said Nasser had announced a major radio address for ten o'clock that night in which he was expected to call for general mobilization in response to the Israeli attack on Khan Yunis. The embassy had told Ambassador Hussein that I was coming and Nasser had asked Hussein to see me as soon as possible after I arrived. I was to see Hussein at 8:00. In the meantime we would see Ambassador Byroade, who was hosting a party near the pyramids but who would meet us at the Mena House nearby. Byroade was deeply disturbed. The U.S. had counseled patience and a prompt acceptance of the deescalation measures developed by General Burns, but since the reinstituted Khan Yunis raid Nasser did not seem to be in a mood to listen. Byroade thought that my discussion with Hussein would be crucial.

Ambassador Hussein was obviously relieved to see me. He said Nasser was in a meeting with his close aides but had asked Hussein to see me and report back as soon as possible. The Prime Minister had authorized an announcement of a radio address later that evening and a mobilization order was one of the things being discussed in the Revolutionary Council. He asked what word I could bring from Israel.

I told him of the cancellation of the earlier raid—based on my report on the initial Cairo discussions. I described the mounting bloody fedayeen depredations over the following two days, and explained the Israeli leaders' eagerness to stop all cross-border violence, as well as the interest of both Sharett and Ben-Gurion in getting onto a new negotiating track. I gave him my assessment that Ben-Gurion, as well as Sharett, was now genuinely interested in pursuing these possibilities. Ambassador Hussein said he thought he had enough to work with. He called me at the hotel a little later to say that the ten o'clock radio broadcast had been cancelled. There would be no mobilization. He would arrange for me to see Nasser the next day. Subsequently that meeting was set for 7:00 P.M.

Nasser and I met again at the Revolutionary Command headquarters. Much of the reserve he had shown in the previous meeting was now gone. He was cordial, relaxed, and unhurried. I emphasized that the Israelis wanted very much to end the cycle of violence and I explained the background of the cancellation of the Israeli raid. He said his men had been most surprised by the pullback of the Israeli forces after they had crossed the demarcation line. He was glad to know that I had something to do with it. He had accepted General Burns's first ceasefire order, but now, after the Khan Yunis attack, he did not know how he would reply to Burns's subsequent letter. He said it was difficult for him to give firm assurance on infiltration but he would do his best to control it. Frequently the fedayeen were out of touch with their leaders for several days at a time. He implied that that was what had happened during the past week when we were all presumably trying to calm the situation. He responded favorably to my suggestion of a separation of forces along the demarcation lines and, to my surprise, said he would be willing to agree to barriers being set up at points of frequent crossing. But he was not prepared to meet either of the Israeli leaders for a direct discussion of ceasefire or armistice questions. This type of question must, he said, be handled through General Burns.

I asked whether he would be interested in meeting Sharett or Ben-Gurion for a discussion of other questions. I told him of Ben-Gurion's suggestion that he would be willing to meet with him anywhere—including in Cairo—for a discussion of basic issues. He seemed initially to be intrigued with the idea. We talked about venue, timing, and possible agenda. He speculated on whether the flexibility the Israeli leaders had shown in our first discussions would continue in any negotiations in which he might engage directly. Would progress be sufficient to permit him to carry other Arab states with him? What would be the risk that, once the negotiations were under way, the Israelis would embarrass him with military attacks—as they had in the Paris talks earlier in the year? This part of our discussion concluded with more questions than answers, but he seemed to gain confidence from a thorough review of the options. He did not close the door on Ben-Gurion's proposal.

I told him I had been reading the Koran and had come across the observation that "Allah is with the steadfast." His face brightened. He said he used to read the Koran but had not read so much recently. He would send me a copy through Ambassador Hussein.

I reminded him that he had expressed an interest in meeting President Eisenhower. He confirmed his strong interest and said a U.S. visit could take place "anytime now." But a little later in the discussion he said it might not take place before February or March. He then turned reflective, saying there were several kinds of imperialism, but "the worst kind is communist." He said he had never been attracted to communism: there "is too much difference between theory and practice." He said he was basically concerned about building a healthy economy in Egypt.

Rumors had persisted in Jerusalem and Cairo that Nasser was, despite what he was saying to me and to others about the communist system, negotiating with Eastern European countries about a major new arms supply. From comments made both by Ambassador Byroade and by Nasser it was evident that the latter's arms supply discussions with the United States were making no progress. I sensed that Nasser was reluctant to turn to the Eastern bloc for any substantial underpinning of his economy or defense forces. But an arms supply agreement with Eastern Europe was an obvious fallback option, and that only emphasized the importance of the current talks—mounted to see if some form of settlement or modus vivendi with Israel was possible, thus removing the justification for a major new arms buildup.

Deciding that the time had come to enlarge the context of our discussion, I suggested that I was just beginning to learn about the larger and more dynamic aspects of the Middle East. Nasser said we should have a long talk about it after my next visit to Israel.

I had a feeling that time was running out, and that the exploration under way must move quickly, either into direct discussions of some sort or into the consecutive heads of state meetings with President Eisenhower suggested earlier by the United States. Under this proposal, which had been under informal consideration during the late summer, President Eisenhower would meet in Washington first with Nasser, followed in two or three weeks by a meeting with Sharett or Ben-Gurion, in an effort to find new common ground. My sense was that the Israeli-Egyptian direct discussion proposal needed one more round of consideration in Jerusalem and Cairo. If that did not produce major results, the Eisenhower proposal was a possibility for keeping the peace process going. So I told Nasser I would make one more trip to Israel and would be back in Cairo at the end of the week. Depending on the discussions I might decide then to return to New York.

Nasser said he would ask Ambassador Hussein to get the list of possible prisoners for exchange to me before I left for Jerusalem. He said he would look forward to our next discussion.

I met Ambassador Hussein later in the evening, Ambassador Byroade the next morning, and Foreign Minister Fawzi in the afternoon. All were grateful that hostilities had subsided and were generous in their comments about how the negotiations had been handled. None of the three, however, was clear about next steps. I concluded that the U.S. proposal for meetings with Eisenhower had encountered snags and did not have clear sailing. This was good reason for a further round of discussion on Ben-Gurion's suggestions for an Israeli-Egyptian face-to-face meeting. I sensed some differences between Byroade's and Washington's approach to the Eisenhower proposal. I was not under State Department appointment and thus not privy to the diplomatic cables on the subject. Thus I did not know precisely what the problem was. But I suspected that a resolution of the difficulty might require discussions in Washington.

The discussions with Fawzi and Hussein confirmed my decision about travel during the following ten days. While I was in Israel on the second trip, Meado Zaki had flown to Damascus to see Egyptian Ambassador Riad. Now Riad, who, like Hussein, was a close colleague of Nasser's, was in Cairo. Before I left for Cyprus, Meado and I met with Riad and Hussein. As I left Cairo, we felt we had Ambassador Riad's support for a resumption of negotiation on basic issues.

During the stay overnight in Cyprus, I enlisted the help of Abraham Kidron, Israeli Counsul General, to pass a message along to Gideon Rafael that Nasser had clearly been a restraining influence on any military activity during the preceding four days, that the Egyptians had accepted General Burns's first call for a ceasefire and were considering his subsequent letter, that Nasser was prepared to hold discussions on armistice adherence questions only through General Burns, and that I would return to Cairo at the end of the week for further discussion with Nasser on Arab-Israeli and other questions.

As I returned to the Nicosia airport the following morning for the short flight to Tel Aviv, the British security forces examined my travel documents in elaborate detail. This was my third Tel Aviv-Cairo trip by way of Cyprus, and the British officers were now aware that something unusual was afoot. I was first separated out from the others waiting to board the plane, then interrogated at some length by the officer in charge. It was only after all the others had enplaned and the plane's engines started that I was permitted to board. I concluded that it would be prudent, if the discussions were to remain confidential, to find a new route for travel. After my second visit the Israelis had issued instructions to all of their border crossing posts that I was to be admitted at any time. This included the post on the Lebanese border and kilometer 95 on the Gaza demarcation line. But principal travel into and out of Israel was by way of the Mandelbaum Gate or the airport at Tel Aviv. The next trip might need to be Tel Aviv to Athens to Cairo.

Gideon Rafael met me at Tel Aviv and we drove to Jerusalem. I was soon in a meeting with Prime Minister Sharett, Rafael, and Jacob Hertzog. I told them of the rapidly moving developments in Cairo after my arrival: the cancellation of the radio broadcast, the Egyptian agreement to the ceasefire, and the long and candid talks with Nasser and his associates. I elaborated on the impressions I had passed on briefly through Abraham Kidron, explaining that Nasser had clearly been a restraining influence in the previous few days but that he wished to handle armistice adherence questions through General Burns and not directly. We discussed Nasser's agreement to a separation of forces, and even to barriers at points on the Gaza demarcation line where crossings frequently took place. I suggested that while I had proposed these two deescalation measures, I did not feel I was the one to conclude the agreements, in view of Nasser's conviction that he and the Israelis should use General Burns for all armistice matters. I told them of Nasser's assertion that he would do his best to control infiltration into Israel, but of his apparent difficulties in view of the loose chain of fedayeen command. Much later I learned that following Nasser's order for a cessation of fedayeen attacks into Israel from the Gaza Strip, other orders were given by the fedayeen command for an escalation of attacks from Jordan. Whether Nasser knew of these subsequent orders I do not know.

We discussed in some detail Nasser's response to Ben-Gurion's proposal for a face-to-face meeting. Sharett was clearly in favor of a "summit meeting." He did not venture an opinion as to whether he or Ben-Gurion should represent Israel.

Sharett showed me a copy of the letter he had originally drafted with the thought he would ask me to carry it to Nasser.* But he said he had decided it was better to let me handle the crisis in my own way. I told Sharett that Nasser had promised a list of prisoners for exchange for me to bring to Jerusalem, and of Dr. Fawzi's subsequent message that, while the exchange had been approved in principle, the list would not be ready until I returned to Cairo.

The next morning I met with General Burns, reporting on the ceasefire and armistice-supporting discussions in Cairo. On the separation of forces, he said he would probably need some help from the U.S. in getting the Israelis to agree to pull back their patrols from the demarcation lines.

That evening I met with Ben-Gurion at his home. He was in bed with a slight temperature. Jacob Hertzog and Colonel Argov were present. Again I reviewed the actions in Cairo after my arrival, including Nasser's final acceptance of Burns's calls for a ceasefire, and his willingness to agree to a greater separation of forces and to physical barriers on the demarcation lines. At the end of this part of the discussion Ben-Gurion said, "So you stopped the war!" I emphasized it had been a "team effort." He laughed and asked what was next.

We talked again about the possibilities of a face-to-face meeting with Nasser for a discussion of basic issues. Ben-Gurion was still

*See Appendix II for draft of letter from Prime Minister Sharett to Prime Minister Nasser, August 31, 1955.

keen for such a meeting and suggested that it take place at kilometer 95 on the Gaza demarcation line. I told him of Nasser's hesitations. Ben-Gurion urged me to explore the possibility further. He thought such a meeting could open entirely new possibilities—not only in Israeli-Egyptian relations but for the whole Middle East. The agenda could be flexible. It could start a "wholly new process" in the resolution of basic issues. While I had become doubtful that such a meeting could be arranged, I agreed to explore the possibilities further.

Ben-Gurion asked if I would be coming back. I said that would depend on the further discussions in Cairo. In any case I would expect to see Prime Minister Sharett in New York early in the UN General Assembly session.

Before leaving for Cairo the next day I had a final meeting in Tel Aviv with Sharett, Rafael, and Hertzog. It was a stock-taking session. They were clear the mission to date had been very useful. A crisis that seemed destined to escalate out of control had been defused. Two new armistice-supporting measures—a further separation of forces and physical barriers on the demarcation line—had been agreed to in principle. The possibility of a face-to-face meeting between senior Israeli and Egyptian leaders was still under serious consideration.

I asked Prime Minister Sharett for his feelings about the U.S. invitation for separate Israeli and Egyptian leadership discussions with President Eisenhower. He said they were interested, although I could see that there would be some question as to whether he or Ben-Gurion would participate—perhaps more uncertainty than over the question of who would participate for Israel in any direct discussions with Nasser. Ben-Gurion clearly saw himself in any such meeting with the Egyptian leader. The mood of the meeting was that progress had been made during the month, that the leadership in both countries probably needed a few weeks for things to settle down following the close brush with major hostilities, after which time the discussions would resume—possibly in New York during the UN General Assembly. In the meantime an exchange of prisoners might be worked out. If Nasser should be responsive to the further discussions about a face-to-face meeting, or indeed to any other principal aspect of our discussions, I would get word to Sharett promptly. We agreed, at the minimum, that Sharett, Rafael, and I would meet late in September in New York. After bringing Ambassador Lawson up to date on the discussions, I left Tel Aviv for Cairo—this time by way of Athens.

A night in Athens was not my idea of how to use time at this point in the negotiations. But neither did it seem prudent to invite further questioning by the British in Cyprus or to ask for additional special privilege from the Jordanians for another eastward trip through Mandelbaum. Fortunately there was an early flight the next morning from Athens to Cairo.

Meado Zaki brought me up to date and we were soon in meetings with Parker Hart, at the embassy, and then with Ambassador Hussein. Both men were still recovering from the unsettling events of the past few days. Neither was clear that negotiations on basic issues could be resumed promptly. They thought the next meeting with Nasser would be decisive on that question. Ambassador Hussein said Nasser was away in the western desert for a few days' holiday with his family. It might thus be four or five days before he would be back and I could see him. It was now September 9, and it was indeed five days before the appointment could be held.

Nasser and I met again at the Revolutionary Command headquarters. Again we were alone. He was tanned and in an ebullient mood. He talked about his family and the importance of spending time with them. He said his usual regimen was to see people in the morning, spend time with his family in the afternoon, and then work late—often until two or three o'clock in the morning.

I told him I appreciated the book on the Koran that he had sent through Ambassador Hussein.* He said he had asked about an English translation of the Koran but was told that there was no really good one. So he thought it was better to send me the commentary on the Koran.

He asked if I had received from Ambassador Hussein the list of prisoners for the proposed exchange. Then before I could answer

---

*Ahmad A. Galwash, *The Religion of Islam* (New York: The Hafner Publishing Company, 1940).

that I had not, he said he understood that I had brought a list from Jerusalem. I showed it to him and told him a little about it. He commented that it had no Egyptians on it. I agreed but pointed out several persons from Sinai and Gaza. He said the trials of the Israeli prisoners in Cairo had been widely publicized. In contrast the people on the Israeli list were unknown in Egypt. He said the Israeli list would be very helpful when the time came for exchange but he thought that, following the hostilities of the past three weeks, a little quiet was needed before the exchange was finally worked out.

I mentioned the need for a reduction of tension in the Gulf of Aqaba. He said he had worked out something on that through the Paris negotiations a few months previously but implied that that plan had collapsed at the time those negotiations were suspended.

I told Nasser of Ben-Gurion's renewed suggestion about a meeting between them at kilometer 95 on the Gaza demarcation line. We again discussed the pros and cons at some length, but he finally settled on the need for a period of quiet before anything like that was attempted. I told him I thought one of the important parts of my last trip to Jerusalem had been my report of the restraint he was now exercising on cross-border violence, and my suggestion that this was a sign of his strength. I said I thought Sharett had had confidence in my exploration from the beginning. But I now felt Ben-Gurion also had confidence. I thought the latter was now convinced something could be worked out on the basic issues— thus his strong interest in a direct discussion to get things started. Nasser did not appear hostile to the idea, just firm that the Khan Yunis raid, when it was finally made, was sufficiently severe that a little time was needed for things to cool down. He said that with his new instructions to the fedayeen and the cancellation of his broadcast he had already started that process.

I shifted the discussion, telling him that I had been reading his book *Egypt's Liberation.* I had been especially interested in the part in which he described the attempted assassination one night of one of King Farouk's associates—an attack in which he had participated—and of his relief the next morning when he found the victim had survived. My interest unleashed a wellspring of recollection and reflection. He said after the attack that night he had gotten no sleep—for the man's cries as he slumped, badly wounded, on his porch, and his wife's and children's cries as they tried to help him rang in his ears all night long. He prayed that the man would not die. He decided that he never again would participate in an assassination attempt and that the revolution would henceforth be bloodless. He said the victim had later been made Minister of Defense by King Farouk. It was such an inappropriate choice that the army then united behind the revolutionary forces and the King was toppled in a bloodless transition. He thought that the revolution would probably not have been possible if the man had died as a result of the assassination attempt. Our discussion of the incident, the book, and his philosophical outlook was a long one. It was clear that I had touched deep wells in both his past experience and in his current interests. He said he had wanted to write a longer book with three more chapters and that he might still write them.

Against the background of our excursion into personal philosophy, I returned the discussion to ways of making progress on Middle Eastern issues. He had felt things must cool down before he could respond to Ben-Gurion's proposal, but, I asked, what about prompt, separate meetings of Egyptian and Israeli leaders with President Eisenhower? He said he was very interested and hoped it would work out but it was again apparent that obstacles had arisen. He said if he came to the U.S. he would want to see me.

Nasser expressed warm appreciation for my efforts, saying he thought they had been very useful—in helping contain the threatened escalation of violence and in helping define several of the areas in which basic accommodations could be made. "Was it five trips I had made," he asked, "between Jerusalem and Cairo?" I confirmed that it was, three by way of Cyprus, one by way of Jordan, and one via Athens. He said he had had word from one of his intelligence men in Jordan that I had gone into Israel from Jordan and then come back through Mandelbaum and gone to Egypt. He was glad to know that their reporting was so accurate!

It had been a long meeting. He had not shown an interest in

talking about larger Middle Eastern issues. It was possible that he really did need a period of freedom from violence in border areas before he entered into further consideration of basic issues. If so, it was time for at least a pause in the talks begun in August. But it was also possible that other negotiations of a fundamental character—probably with Eastern Europe—were coming to a head. Whatever the situation, it was obvious prompt consultations were needed in Philadelphia and Washington.

After talking the next day with Ambassadors Hussein and Byroade, I left for New York. Hussein was gloomy but we agreed to meet promptly in Washington. Ambassador Byroade shared Hussein's pessimism. It was apparent that the U.S. invitation to the Israeli and Egyptian leaders to come to the United States for separate discussions with Eisenhower had not been unconditional invitations. Certain advance commitments were being asked—at least of Nasser. The latter was prepared for a candid, across-the-board discussion, but he did not like the idea of making commitments in advance of the talks. Rumors continued about a possible arms deal with Eastern Europe. The long flight from Cairo to New York seemed endless.

The Israelis did not know the results of my final discussions in Cairo. So on arrival in New York I called Ambassador Kidron, and then met with Jacob Blaustein. I reported to my colleagues in Philadelphia and then on Thursday, September 22, met with George Allen in Washington. Mr. Allen was emphatic that Washington had not intended that there should be any conditions on President Eisenhower's invitation to Nasser to visit the United States. He erupted with anger that some, apparently, had been attached somewhere in the chain of command. Rumors of an impending Egyptian-Eastern European arms deal were circulating in Washington and Nasser, indeed, had just notified Ambassador Byroade of such an accord. George Allen agreed that the proposed Eisenhower-Nasser discussions, followed by Eisenhower-Sharett/Ben-Gurion talks, appeared to be the only means by which, in Nasser's eyes, the peace process could continue as a viable alternative to a major new arms supply.

Secretary of State John Foster Dulles was out of town, Eisenhower was on vacation in Colorado, and it was unclear how fast the U.S. could move to straighten things out with Cairo. On Tuesday, September 27, Nasser announced the Egyptian-Czechoslovakian agreement, in which Egyptian cotton was to be exchanged for Czechoslovakian arms. The shock in Washington and in European capitols was seismic.

Following Nasser's announcement, Washington decided to send George Allen to Cairo. Secretary Dulles was deeply disturbed over Nasser's action, and press reports spread that Allen would be carrying a U.S. ultimatum to Nasser. Ambassador Byroade attempted as best he could to dispel these reports in Cairo, but Nasser was in no mood to receive a lecture. When Allen arrived on the morning of September 30 he was told it would not be possible to see Nasser that day. The following day President Nasser kept Allen and Byroade waiting for an hour and a half before he saw them. When the meeting finally took place, Nasser completely rejected any suggestion that he alter his announced course.

IV ⟋

The Political and
Security Context

BEFORE ATTEMPTING TO assess the deeper meaning of the
Egyptian-Israeli negotiations it might be useful to look at the developments in the Middle East from 1950 onward that provided the
political and security backdrop.

The principal elements in that political tapestry were:

- Continuing consultations between Britain, France, and the
  United States under the 1950 Tripartite Declaration, in which
  the three countries attempted from 1950 to 1954 to prevent the
  outbreak of war in the area through a rationing of armaments
  to the countries directly involved in the Arab-Israeli conflict.

- The initial assessment of the United States government that the
  new revolutionary government in Egypt was strongly nationalist
  in orientation, would be firm in its administration, and would
  continue a generally pro-Western policy.

- The desire of Washington, nevertheless, to give general support
  to the British effort to get what they considered to be an accept-

able Suez settlement. The U.S. was thus responsive to British objections to any U.S. arms assistance to Cairo.

- The determination of the new revolutionary government in Cairo to maintain its independence. This meant that Cairo found unacceptable most of the conditions on arms aid proposed by the United States, including proposals that Egypt participate in a regional security structure in the Middle East.

- During the year previous to the Egyptian-Czech arms agreement Israel continued to build up her military forces. Arms supply negotiations continued—in particular, with France, with initial deliveries being made in 1955.

- Nasser's frustration over his difficulties in getting arms from the West, his attendance at the Bandung Conference in April 1955, and his discussions there with Nehru and Chou En-lai greatly increased his interest in a policy of nonalignment.

- Following the conclusion in July 1954 of the British-Egyptian preliminary agreement on British withdrawal from Suez and the final agreement in October of that year, the Egyptian and Israeli governments both felt their armed forces were becoming very exposed. After the Israeli attack on Gaza on February 28, 1955, Prime Minister Nasser became especially concerned either to get a settlement with Israel or to arrange for major new arms supply.

THE ROCKY ROAD TO EGYPTIAN NONALIGNMENT

Very shortly after the cessation of Egyptian-Israeli hostilities in 1949 under the UN-sponsored Armistice Agreements negotiated by Ralph Bunche, the Cairo government approached both London and Washington for arms supply for its military forces, greatly weakened as a result of the Palestine war. Britain responded with an agreement for limited supplies, but with increasing British-Egyptian strains over the Suez Canal base, supply was largely suspended.

Egyptian requests to the United States met with the general

parry that in these matters Egypt was essentially within the British sphere. It was suggested, however, that any U.S. response would in the end be determined by Cairo's pro-Western stance and its willingness to participate in some form of regional defense. The first such regional proposal, one for a Middle East Command headquartered on the Suez Canal, had been proposed by the British in 1951 and was rejected by the prerevolutionary Wafd government in Cairo as an all too transparent attempt to keep British forces in the Canal area.

Egypt again approached Washington, early in 1952, with the hope that it could secure internal security equipment. While an agreement was reached for Cairo to purchase $5 million of equipment, none had been delivered by July 23, 1952, when Nasser and his Free Officers took over the government.

It was Ali Sabry, a close associate of Nasser's, who immediately following the revolution got in touch with the U.S. and who, after the new government had received a positive assessment in Washington and some encouragement from U.S. defense officials, came to Washington late in November 1952 with a refined shopping list. Cairo had been led to believe that as much as $100 million of arms equipment might be available. After arrival in Washington, Sabry found the figure to be nearer $10 million, with even that tied to a settlement of the dispute over the British base on the Canal. Ultimately the U.S. withdrew entirely from the negotiations—leaving the new Egyptian government considerably disillusioned. Later, in 1955, Ali Sabry was to be one of those close to Nasser who was most active in pressing for Soviet arms.

This early experience was only the first of a series of arms negotiations between the new government and the U.S. that came to naught.*

The British continued to oppose U.S. arms aid to Egypt and in June 1954 Washington assured London that the U.S. would not provide arms aid to Cairo until there was a final settlement between

*For an excellent review of these negotiations see Paul Jabber, *Not by War Alone: Security and Arms Control in the Middle East* (Berkeley: University of California Press, 1981).

Britain and Egypt over Suez. In July Washington assured Cairo that with a Suez settlement the U.S. would extend both military and economic assistance. In November, following the conclusion of the Suez agreement, Washington, in response to the July pledge, offered Cairo $27 million in military aid and $13 million in economic aid. But the terms under which the military aid would be provided were in contention through the spring and summer of 1955. Nasser was not prepared to accept the Military Assistance Advisory Group (MAAG) that the U.S. wished to send. Other questions arose over restrictions on the use of weapons as provided for in the Mutual Security Act. But in the background, even after the Suez settlement, there was continuing British pressure that the U.S. not provide arms to Egypt and a U.S. belief that Cairo really had nowhere else to go for weapons supply.

While the revolutionary government in Cairo initially showed an interest in some form of regional security arrangement, as the Suez negotiations proceeded with the British, Cairo's interest in any regional arrangement waned. With the conclusion of the Suez accord, Secretary Dulles's interest turned to the possibility of a regional security pact among the so-called northern tier of countries with frontiers bordering on Russia—Turkey, Iraq, Iran, and Pakistan. He saw a linking of these countries filling the gap between NATO on the west and the Southeast Asian Treaty Organization (SEATO) on the east. While the "northern tier" proposal was initiated with some hope that it would include other countries of the Middle East, Nasser saw the proposal as divisive and campaigned vigorously against any Arab participation. Iraq was the only such state to join. The other Arab states saw Israel as providing a greater threat than the Soviet Union. It was a situation with many parallels to that faced today in attempts to develop any regional defense structure. The rift in approach between Cairo and Washington over these and related issues continued to complicate negotiations over arms aid right up to September 1955, when Nasser announced the Egyptian-Czech arms agreement.

During this period a very modest level of U.S. economic assistance was continued, largely as a result of nurturing by Ambassador Hussein. But there was no suggestion from either Washington or

Cairo that the difficulties in achieving an arms agreement be bypassed and bilateral relations be undergirded by a general program of large-scale economic assistance. That kind of proposal was only made by the U.S. in connection with the financing of the Aswan Dam in an effort to salvage the situation after the Egyptian-Czech arms agreement.

At various times during the prolonged and inconclusive arms negotiations with Washington in the year prior to the Czech accord, Nasser had suggested to both British and American negotiators that if no agreement was obtained he might need to seek arms from the Soviet Union. No one in Washington took these suggestions very seriously. Opinions differ as to exactly when "basic negotiations" began with the Eastern Europeans. But it is clear that Nasser's motivation greatly increased as a result of the Israeli attack on Gaza on February 28, 1955. The attack was the largest military operation carried out against territory under Egyptian control since the Palestine war. There were eighty-five Egyptian casualties, with forty soldiers killed.

Nasser was also deeply disturbed by reports in the spring of 1955 of negotiations for future delivery of French planes, tanks, and other advanced equipment to Israel, supplemented by British tanks provided through French dealers. He suspected U.S. and U.K. complicity. But in any case the tripartite system was no longer a restraint.

Nasser had been invited to attend the Bandung Conference of Non-Aligned countries in Indonesia in April. In March he made an effort to get final and acceptable terms for the $27 million military aid from the United States. He was informed that payment would be expected in cash but otherwise received no answer before he left Cairo on April 9 for Bandung. Nasser had long been an admirer of Prime Minister Nehru and the conference enabled him to become very much better acquainted with both Nehru and Chou En-lai, each of whom had taken a leadership role in organizing the conference. The Egyptian leader gained stature from his participation at Bandung and Chou, in a decidedly pre-Russian-Chinese split suggestion, offered to take up with the Soviets the question of arms supply. Nasser was sufficiently encouraged by these developments to discuss them with a close circle of his advisors on his return to Cairo. A subsequent exchange with Daniel Solod, the Soviet Ambassador in Cairo, confirmed Moscow's interest.

Armed with the Soviet response Nasser, who still basically preferred American arms aid, told Ambassador Byroade on June 9 that unless the U.S. was more responsive to recent requests he would turn to the Eastern bloc. While senior officials in Washington regarded Nasser's démarche as bluff they did permit Ambassador Byroade to tell the Egyptians that they would permit them to purchase arms and suggested they make a specific request. Egypt did so on June 30. Cairo was informed that some of the materials were available and that others were not; but any sales must be paid for promptly and in dollars. The available items would cost $27 million. While Cairo was not without some dollar resources it was reluctant to exhaust these and suggested part payment in cotton or Egyptian currency.* When Washington failed to agree and responded with silence to Nasser's appeal for a relaxation of the proposed financial terms, he resumed negotiations with the Soviets.

Dimitri Shepilov, a member of the Soviet Central Committee and a close friend of Khrushchev, visited Cairo on July 21 presumably to give the situation one final assessment from the point of view of Soviet interests. Details of a possible arms supply agreement may have been discussed by an Egyptian technical delegation that visited Prague at the end of the month.

But despite the acceleration of Eastern European negotiations, Nasser continued throughout August and early September to query Washington about a change in terms for the aid requested in June in response to the U.S. suggestion. I have mentioned the general expectation in Cairo when I left for New York on September 15 that an arms agreement with Eastern Europe was impending and Nasser's report to Byroade on September 21 that an agreement had been reached.

Three salvage efforts by Washington bore no fruit. On the evening of Friday, September 23, following my report to George Allen the day before, Kermit Roosevelt, who was considered in Washing-

*Discussion with Ambassador Hussein, Cairo, June 23, 1982.

ton to have a close personal relationship with Nasser, was sent to Cairo in an effort to head off the Eastern arms agreement. Believing apparently that it was too late to get Nasser to abort the agreement, Roosevelt's principal effort is reported to have been to get Nasser to moderate his attitude toward Israel.* In a second effort the U.S. on September 25 announced that it would be willing to provide Egypt with arms on credit.

It was not, however, as I have earlier suggested, a good weekend for basic policy decisions. Secretary Dulles was away from Washington and Eisenhower was on a long vacation in Colorado. Dulles's efforts to talk with Eisenhower by phone on September 23 —presumably in part about the Middle East—proved difficult, and the President's substantial emotional upset over being called off the golf course four times for the conclusion of one call with his Secretary of State undoubtedly contributed to his serious heart attack later that night.† The failure of the third salvage effort— George Allen's quick trip to Cairo—only added to Washington's frustration.

Eric Johnston's water negotiations had already encountered major obstacles. The Arab states, under pressure to develop plans for the settlement of Palestine refugees, were determined not to agree to any arrangement that took substantial amounts of water out of the Jordan valley. The Israelis were equally determined to provide water for the settlement of new Jewish emigrants in the Negev. The announcement of the Egyptian-Czech arms agreement effectively ended negotiations that were already reaching a basic impasse.

Nasser's action did not represent a completely loose cannon on the international deck. Over the preceding months he had developed a political model. He had been increasingly attracted by India's policy of nonalignment. Nehru had no basic problem in accepting arms from both East and West, and believed that in the process he was strengthening India's nonaligned position. Nasser

*Donald Neff, *Warriors at Suez* (New York: Simon and Shuster, 1981), p. 89.
†Ibid., pp. 99–100.

and Nehru had generally gotten on well at the Bandung Conference in April and over the summer months of 1955 Egypt had a military mission in India consulting about arms aid. Nasser had just appointed one of his close friends, Mostafa Kamel, as Egyptian Ambassador to New Delhi. Ambassador Kamel was apparently one of a very few members of the Egyptian diplomatic community, beyond those previously mentioned, whom Nasser had drawn into the discussions in Cairo about a possible settlement with Israel.

Thus, when Nasser signed the arms supply agreement with Czechoslovakia, the Indian model was in the forefront of his mind. He did not consider that he was cutting his links with the West. He was frustrated and disillusioned in his arms supply negotiations with the United States and, in the absence of a settlement with Israel, was convinced he must strengthen his military establishment.

Perhaps the best summary of Nasser's views at this point was in a press conference he held on October 5, following the announcement of the Czech agreement.* He said he had informed the United States in June that he would buy arms from the Soviet Union if the United States would not supply them. "It seems they did not believe me," he said. He continued, "I suppose they thought it was a bluff. But it was not a matter for bluffing. I needed the arms and I had no alternative but to supply myself from the East." Washington officials expressed incredulity and asserted that there was no hint in the U.S.-Egyptian arms talks in June that the alternative to arms from the West was arms from the Soviet bloc.†

Washington also suggested that the Egyptian request, which included limited quantities of tanks, aircraft, and artillery, had been approved "in principle." This appeared to mean that if the Egyptians had been able to pay the price, they could have had the arms. But as we have seen, the U.S. had rejected an Egyptian

*New York Times, October 6, 1955.

†The assertion was clearly incorrect. President Eisenhower in his book The White House Years: Waging Peace, 1956–1961 (New York: Doubleday, 1965, p. 25) states that in September 1955, when the Israelis "jarred" Nasser "by executing another strong and successful raid on an Egyptian outpost, he made good his threat of the previous June and took steps to obtain arms from Communist nations."

suggestion that arms payments be made partially in cotton or in local currency. They had insisted on immediate payment in dollars —something that would have largely drained Egypt's reserves.

In the ninety-minute press conference, Nasser said "Egypt had no aggressive intentions toward Israel." He emphasized that Egypt's urgent need for weapons was based not so much on Israel's present military preponderance as on evidence that her arms lead over the Arab states had increased and would increase further over the coming year. He then gave specifics of what he said were several Israeli forward purchases.

Nasser was asked if Egypt would attack Israel if victory appeared easy and certain. He replied, "War is not an easy decision for anybody, especially for me. No Arab is saying now that we must destroy Israel. The Arabs are asking only that refugees [from Palestine] receive their natural right to life and their lost property which was promised them by United Nations resolutions seven years ago." "No," he said, "we are not aggressive. The threat is from the other side. I have said many times that I want to build up my country. Now I am obliged to give defense priority over development." "It was," he continued, "the other way around before Ben-Gurion's vicious attack on Gaza February 28." "I cannot defend Egypt," he said, "with schools and hospitals and factories, and what will be the use of them if they are destroyed?" Commenting on Ben-Gurion's statement the week before that there were "no essential differences between Israel and Egypt," the depth of Nasser's anger over the February raid at a time when informal negotiations were continuing was further emphasized when he said, "February 28 and what came after it are the issues between Egypt and Israel." Nasser went on to say that the Egyptian-Czech agreement would "make Israel think twice about aggressive actions." He said he had been expecting another large-scale attack ever since February 28 but he thought the danger would decrease as the Arab-Israeli arms balance was restored. Asked whether Egypt would allow the dispute over the Gulf of Aqaba to be submitted to the International Court for arbitration, he replied, "That question will take some thinking."

Queried at the press conference about relations between the

Arab bloc and the United States, Nasser said these relations were passing through a critical state. "The initiative for development of future relations is completely with the United States," he said. "The Arabs do not insist on better treatment than that accorded Israel. Equal treatment will come about," he asserted, "if the United States acts purely in its own interest and does not pay special attention to interests favored by a small minority of Americans." Asked whether he preferred the West or the East as his armaments source, he said, "For years we tried to supply ourselves from our accustomed sources in the West, but we failed. Why? Because there was a sort of monopoly. The West felt that they could give us or not give us whatever they liked because they thought they were our only market. . . . For three years we waited and tried. There was an arms race going on, but it was one-sided. Israel was running and we were standing still."

In response to a question in the press conference about the possibility of admitting Soviet bloc technicians, he said, "I do not think there will be any need for foreign technicians to look after the Czech arms. We have a group of the best technicians in the world among our own people. . . . We have excellent technical training centers here."

Egypt did not appear to be headed toward anything like the role of a Soviet satellite, but it was clear that she had shifted sharply toward a more formal type of neutralism.

Many senior U.S. officials in Washington had believed Nasser was bluffing. They underestimated both his determination and his independence. The Bandung Conference had brought him in closer touch with world leaders, had widened his horizon, and had strengthened substantially his interest in nonalignment. He made it clear in mid-August in our first meeting in Cairo that he was disillusioned with his arms supply negotiations with the U.S. On several occasions we had talked about India and nonalignment. He and his associates attributed much of their difficulty to what they considered to be the general hostility of John Foster Dulles. They felt he had little understanding of the Egyptian revolution or of the implications of the Bandung Conference. Ambassador Hussein, who got on well with Dulles, was the exception. But despite the

Ambassador's efforts, and those of George Allen, the Assistant Secretary of State, who was an experienced diplomat and well acquainted with the Middle East, U.S. and Egyptian policies continued during the spring and summer to run on parallel tracks—without an effective dialogue. Senior officials in Washington were just not prepared to believe that Nasser was serious about looking elsewhere for arms supply.

Primary public attention in the U.S., as far as the Middle East was concerned, was focused on Eric Johnston's water negotiations, which had stirred a great deal of international interest. Late in the summer the U.S. developed the proposal for Israeli and Egyptian leaders to come to Washington, several weeks apart, for discussion with President Eisenhower. But, as I have suggested earlier, there was confusion as to whether the Washington invitation was unconditional or whether advance commitments were being asked. The failure to clarify these questions more promptly was in itself an indication of lassitude and uncertainty in U.S. policy.

There were major differences in approach within Nasser's cabinet and inner circle. Over the spring and summer he had given considerable negotiating leeway to Ali Sabry and others in the cabinet who favored an Eastern European arms supply agreement. But it was clear to me the final decisions were being kept firmly in his own hands. Through my second visit to Cairo he was still talking in meaningful terms about ways in which he could reach a basic settlement with Israel. He was still weighing Ben-Gurion's proposal for a meeting. But after talking with Nasser on the third visit in the second week of September, it was clear that only the direct involvement of President Eisenhower could bring the kind of dramatic progress in the Egyptian-Israeli negotiations that might forestall a major Egyptian-East European arms accord—and it was then very, very late.

It had been a rocky road from the first approach to the U.S. by Ali Sabry on behalf of the Free Officers group immediately following the revolution in July 1952 to Nasser's announcement on September 27, 1955 of the Czech arms deal. But the years following were to be no less difficult, and fifteen years later, in July 1970, shortly before he died, Nasser was to suggest to Anwar el-Sadat that Soviet-Egyptian relations were a "hopeless case."*

ISRAEL: QUESTIONS OF SECURITY AND LEADERSHIP

While the Egyptian, Jordanian, and Syrian forces had acquitted themselves with some success during the hostilities immediately following the passage of the United Nations resolution partitioning Palestine, by the summer of 1948 the Israeli forces, invigorated by the reality of their dream of a Jewish state, had rolled the Arab armies back from a part of the territory they had occupied following their declaration of war on the new state of Israel. By the time Ralph Bunche had achieved the Armistice Agreements in 1949, the Arab forces were heavily depleted.

Britain had supplied arms to Cairo in 1949 and 1950 but with the British, French, and U.S. agreement on the Tripartite Declaration of 1950 Israel did not have reason to be unduly concerned with her general security position. In October 1951, Egypt denounced the 1936 Treaty of Alliance with Britain and in response Britain largely suspended arms supply. However, with the emergence in 1952 of the Revolutionary Government in Cairo, and its interest in resolving the impasse on the Anglo-Egyptian Condominium over the Sudan, Britain offered to provide Egypt with fighter aircraft. Israel was to receive a slightly larger number and other planes were to go to Lebanon, Syria, and Iraq. Israel's strong representations over what it considered to be the imbalance of the proposal ultimately bore some fruit and it was able eventually to purchase double the number originally proposed. By 1953 only four planes had reached Egypt and, with British-Egyptian relations becoming strained over the Suez base issue, deliveries were finally completely suspended.

During the years 1950 to 1954 the United States preferred to stay out of arms supply to all the countries of the Middle East. Small-scale assistance was provided to Iran, Iraq, and Jordan, but, as I

*Anwar el-Sadat, *In Search of Identity* (New York: Harper Colophon Books, Harper and Row, 1979), p. 128.

have suggested earlier, Washington preferred to let Britain take the lead. Such a policy reflected both President Eisenhower's respect for Britain and his desire to give the British general support in their negotiations with Egypt over their base on the Suez Canal. With the British force of 80,000 on the Canal, Israel had a sense of security.

While the British interest was to retain influence in the area, the French concern was to try to regain an influence that had been lost. Nevertheless, except for a small shipment of arms to Syria in 1949–50 and the sale in 1950 of some war surplus planes to Israel, there was no substantial transfer of arms to the area by France until 1955.*

However, beginning in 1950 the Israelis and the French had begun to develop a close arms relationship, looking to future cooperation. Initially the Quai d'Orsay was cool to the development, but the Ministry of Defense, prominent persons on the political left, and business interests closely connected with the armaments industry gave increasingly strong support.

In 1952 a French proposal to sell jet fighters to Israel was turned down under the Tripartite Agreement, but in August 1954, working in secret and without consultation with Britain and the U.S., the French and Israelis undertook negotiations on a large arms sale agreement that included jet planes, tanks, and artillery. Negotiations continued in 1955 with deliveries to follow later in the year. The flow was to be accelerated following Nasser's announcement of the arms agreement with Czechoslovakia.

The Israeli-French arms negotiations reflected an increased general sense of insecurity in Israel following the initialing in July 1954 of an agreement between London and Cairo for the British evacuation from Suez. Not only was there a new, vigorous, and strongly nationalist government in Cairo, but there was now to be no third-party buffer between Egypt and Israel. In subsequent years, the buffer role was to be played by a United Nations Emergency Force, stationed in the Sinai, and, under the 1979 Israeli-Egyptian Peace

*See Jabber, *Not by War Alone* pp. 99–106, for a more detailed review of British and French negotiations.

Treaty, by a multinational force established by the United Nations Security Council, or if that proved impossible, by a force to be formed by the three signatories of the treaty. Soviet objections to a UN force having prevented the development of a buffer unit, the treaty signatories put together a force composed of military units from the United States, Australia, Britain, Columbia, Fiji, France, Italy, the Netherlands, New Zealand, Norway, and Uruguay.

Word of the French-Israeli arms negotiations became more general knowledge in March 1955—just as Nasser was attempting to cope with the shock and aftereffects of the major Israeli raid on Gaza. The French-Israeli arms negotiations had effectively ended arms control efforts under the Tripartite Declaration. The Declaration became fully obsolete in September with Nasser's announcement of the Czech arms accord.

But arms supply to Israel or to neighboring Arab states was only part of Israel's security problem.

The Armistice Agreements between Israel and Egypt, Jordan, Lebanon, and Syria established armistice lines and provided for their policing by a UN Truce Supervisory Organization (UNTSO) to ensure that there would be no resumption of hostilities.

Perhaps it was too much to hope that a few dozen UNTSO observers could bring quiet to armistice lines separating Arab refugees from homes in which they and their families had lived for years. Terrorist activity was familiar to both the Arab and Jewish communities—both communities in prepartition years having tolerated groups using terrorist tactics. Some Palestinians had been driven from their homes by the actions of one or more of these groups. The UN observers, by their presence and their ability to investigate incidents and their prompt access to army commanders on both sides, were able to deter infiltration and cross-border violence. But motivation for armistice violations was high and quiet did not prevail.

During the early 1950s the number and frequency of Arab terrorist attacks across the armistice lines increased. Such attacks usually left one or more Israeli civilians dead—often innocent women and children—with Israeli opinion inflamed and demanding retribution. In response, the Israelis developed a policy of retaliation against targets identified in most cases as having collaborated in the terrorist activity. The general rationale was that the retaliatory strike would deter the targeted community from permitting terrorist raids to be launched soon again from that area, and would over time cause the Arab state from which the raid emanated either to restrict such activity or to expel the organizing group—as Jordan did with the Palestine Liberation Organization (PLO) in September 1970.

The theory, however, as carried out by the Israeli military, had some fundamental limitations. The retaliatory raids were largely carried out by heavily armed and highly trained commando units of the army, which, despite instructions to avoid large numbers of civilian deaths, usually left heavy civilian casualties and substantial devastation in their wake. The loss of Arab, and at times of Israeli, lives in the raids were often so substantial—and so disproportionate to the loss in the previous marauding activity—that world opinion was shocked and international condemnation of Israel by the UN Security Council or General Assembly usually followed. With each such large-scale retaliatory attack, political support in the international community tended to increase for the Arab cause —and their pleas for more arms fell on progressively receptive ears.

As this basic Israeli security dilemma unfolded it brought new strains within Israeli leadership. Ben-Gurion believed that time would inevitably work to the advantage of the Arab states, as they steadily built up their military capabilities. He believed Israel's security lay in keeping neighboring states "off-balance" by occasional sharp attacks. Such retaliation also had the effect of assuaging Israeli public opinion. Moshe Dayan, who as Chief of Staff shared Ben-Gurion's views, believed that when the Arab states were confident they had a clear preponderance of military power they would lay plans to attack Israel. Israel could then destroy their armies with a decisive preemptive attack. Dayan's approach underwent some changes and he became a voice for a negotiated solution after he took over the Foreign Ministry under Prime Minister Begin in 1977.

Moshe Sharett, who had been Foreign Minister in Ben-Gurion's cabinet from the beginning, and who had to deal with the international repercussions of what many in the international community and some in Israel considered to be disproportionate retaliatory violence, saw more possibilities of a long-term accommodation with the neighboring Arab states.

The differing approaches within the Israeli leadership to these fundamental issues of security policy came to a head in the fall of 1953. Ben-Gurion, tired and in need of rest and reflection, was on leave, and Sharett was deputizing for him. Pinchas Lavon had replaced Sharett as Acting Minister of Defense.

The differences in approach between Ben-Gurion and Sharett, mirroring differing assessments within the Israeli public of future security risks, had already been reflected in Cabinet discussions, where Sharett, even before Ben-Gurion took leave, had occasionally mustered a majority for his point of view. But these differences were now to become more acute.

In mid-October, without Sharett's approval,* Lavon authorized a major raid against Qibya, an Arab village in Jordan, in retaliation for a long list of depredations by infiltrators—but most recently the murder of a mother and her children in an Israeli village near the border. Sixty-six villagers in Qibya, most of them women and children, died in the attack—many in the rubble of their dynamited houses. Another seventy-five were wounded or received severe injuries. Ariel Sharon commanded the Israeli force. The United Nations reacted vigorously with a resolution condemning Israel's action, while censoring Jordan for its violations of the Armistice Agreement. The terrorist action, the Israeli retaliatory response, and the UN action combined to spur terrorist activity generally and to increase Israel's sense of isolation. When challenged by Sharett as to why he had undertaken the action without his consent, Lavon maintained that he had consulted Ben-Gurion in the Negev. Ben-Gurion subsequently stated that he had not approved the operation.

Despite his apprehension that Sharett was not sufficiently tough-minded to take over as Prime Minister, Ben-Gurion in December

*Rafael, *Destination Peace,* p. 33.

relinquished the post to him and with his wife, Paula, retired to the Sde Boker kibbutz in the Negev. Soon the strains in the Israeli government were to be exacerbated by two additional developments.

With progress toward a British-Egyptian agreement for the withdrawal of the British from Suez, and with Israel's sense of insecurity increased by what they considered to be an unwarranted evenhandedness on the part of the U.S., two contradictory lines of approach emerged in the Israeli Cabinet. One group believed that with the British gone Nasser would turn his attention to rebuilding Egypt's economy and would be more open to a settlement with Israel. A second group believed that the implications of British withdrawal were so great for Israel's security that everything possible should be done to thwart a British-Egyptian agreement on Suez. This latter group saw, in the vigorous U.S. support for a complete British evacuation, a currying of favor with Egypt that could only put Israel's future at risk.

Sharett was one who believed there to be some hope that Nasser might be willing to consider settlement possibilities. He thus proposed and Nasser accepted an arrangement for a series of informal exchanges beginning in the autumn of 1954. But other events were to add serious complications.

In the summer of 1954 a series of explosions rocked a number of buildings in Cairo in which British and American offices were located. A group of young Jewish residents of Cairo was arrested and accused of working for Israeli intelligence. Late in September it was announced in Cairo that they would be put on trial. A few days later Sharett found that, without his knowledge, two of his colleagues—Lavon and Colonel Benjamin Gibli, head of military intelligence—had indeed been involved. The theory had apparently been that the acts of sabotage would be attributed to Egyptians and that this discovery would somehow destroy the Suez withdrawal negotiations. It was an extraordinary and embarrassing episode which, together with the effort to keep it under cover, was to dog Israeli politics for years to come.

The surprise is that against this background, Sharett was able to initiate the informal exchange with Nasser—although Nasser did insist that Sharett's efforts to get leniency for the arrested Jewish youths be handled separately from the discussions about more general relationships.

Army morale was understandably low. In February Lavon resigned, and, in an effort to bolster both political and military morale, Ben-Gurion was persuaded to return to the Cabinet as Defense Minister. Subsequently, in November of 1955 Ben-Gurion, having led the field in the July elections, again took over the Prime Ministership.

The fall and early winter months of 1954 had been relatively quiet on the armistice lines. But early in February a number of fedayeen gangs, operating from the Gaza Strip, engaged in depredations and terrorist activity deep inside Israel. Israeli public opinion was inflamed and the military was restive—following extensive public criticism over the Cairo affair. After Ben-Gurion's return to the Cabinet, Sharett authorized the retaliatory strike against Egyptian military strongholds in Gaza—asking Dayan, Chief of Staff, to exercise restraint. As we have seen, the action took place on February 28 with heavy loss of lives.

The series of events that led to my involvement in the Egyptian-Israeli settlement effort in the months just preceding the Egyptian-Czech arms accord began with the Gaza raid and its aftermath.

V ⟶

The Limitations and Advantages of a Nonofficial Role

WHEN AMBASSADOR HUSSEIN first approached Quakers in April 1955, he suggested the State Department's position was that the time was not ripe for official negotiations on basic Middle Eastern issues.

The United States, in fact, late in 1954 had launched an intensive appraisal of the possibilities of bringing about an Arab-Israeli peace settlement. In October Secretary Dulles had appointed Francis H. Russell, who had held a number of State Department posts, including that of Chargé d'Affaires at the U.S. Embassy in Tel Aviv, as a Special Assistant responsible for coordinating activities of the Administration concerning the Palestine question.

Apparently, early in 1955, as a result of Ambassador Russell's activities, it was concluded within the Administration that an Arab-Israeli settlement was possible—given the necessary Great Power initiative and support.

But that was an important qualification. It was probably a combination of elements which led Washington to advise the Egyptians in the spring that the U.S. did not believe the time was right for official negotiations: the belief Eric Johnston's efforts to get a Jordan water settlement would succeed, given a little more time; the difficulties of getting agreement in senior circles in Washington and with the other Great Powers on the nature of any formal negotiations; and a belief that there was no reason to hurry.

Ambassador Hussein and Dr. Fawzi, like Nasser doubtful that U.S. arms would be available, and aware of the Eastern European arms possibility, were deeply concerned that a third option be explored. Because of Nasser's bitter reaction to the February 28 Israeli attack on Gaza in the midst of the Egyptian-Israeli informal negotiations in Paris, they knew a direct Egyptian approach to Israel to resume such negotiations would not at that stage be possible. With the U.S. believing that the time was not right for formal negotiation, Dr. Fawzi and Ambassador Hussein thus turned to a nongovernmental third party in an effort to get something moving. Realizing the enormous stakes involved, they had convinced Nasser that this course of action was worth a try.

It was the fact of Egyptian initiative and the nonofficial character of the proposed exploration—against the background of past Quaker work in the area—which probably caused George Allen and his colleagues in Washington to give it strong support, and to ask the two U.S. ambassadors to cooperate. George Allen recognized that such an informal exploration need not get in the way of Eric Johnston's negotiation or require a major and immediate new decision in the senior levels of the U.S. government—and it just might open up some new possibilities.

Ambassador Hussein's proposal had been skillfully phrased. He suggested that, despite U.S. belief that the time was not right for negotiation, Quakers might be useful in bringing forward a suggested formula which, if agreed to by Israel, would be of great interest to representatives of the Arab States. He emphasized that it was easier for Egypt to respond to suggestions made by others. He felt that if an imaginative formula could be found, that in itself might create the timing for action. It was a proposal that took into account Nasser's sensitivities over the Paris experience and Egypt's relationships with other Arab States. The Egyptians would not be in a position of having to lay the initial proposals on the table, but the fact that they would be known to have initiated the exploration would be an inducement to the Israelis and to the U.S. to take it seriously.

I was an independent third party, and while my efforts were strongly supported by senior U.S. officials, I was not privy to all of the detailed considerations surrounding the proposed invitation from Washington for the leaders of Egypt and Israel to come to the United States—roughly a month apart—for discussions with the President. As suggested earlier, I had learned in mid-August of the general possibility of such an arrangement. The Israeli leaders were interested but preferred that the possibility of a direct face-to-face meeting with Nasser, such as proposed by Ben-Gurion, be explored first. Nasser continued to express confidence in President Eisenhower and an interest in meeting with him, but, as suggested, I became convinced early in September during my second visit to Cairo that Nasser was being asked, in return for the invitation, to make certain advance commitments. He clearly did not like it.

Would the overall outcome have been different if I had been a U.S. official, fully informed of the cable traffic between Washington and Cairo on the U.S. invitation, and expected to make recommendations? The answer is certainly that it would have made a difference.

But other considerations were involved.

Firstly, as I have suggested, U.S. Middle East policy during the spring and summer was in some disarray. Strong conflicting views were held in Washington, and had I been a U.S. official, clear and timely negotiating instructions would have been difficult to obtain. Presumably the Egyptians took this general situation into account in seeking nongovernmental assistance in the exploration of settlement possibilities.

During the Jerusalem-Cairo negotiations I was not aware in detail of the substantive conclusions being developed by Francis Russell and his group until Secretary Dulles summarized them in an address on August 26. The speech, a useful outline of U.S. readiness to assist in a political settlement, outlined pledges of aid in resettlement and repatriation of refugees, delineation of boundaries, and future measures to keep the peace. But it was introduced into a situation facing the possibility of a sea change in political dynamics, and it took no account of the limited options available to the United States to influence the impending course of events. Had Washington been in more effective communication with Cairo, the speech might have provided the peace process with a helpful lift. But given the preoccupations in Jerusalem and Cairo, the speech was quickly lost in a situation which called at that stage not for new settlement ideas but for dramatic action to cut through the delay and confusion which had marked U.S.-Egyptian bilateral relations over the summer. It was a confusion that had engulfed even the invitations to Washington.

Secondly, had a U.S. official been carrying on the exploration, he would almost certainly have found that his discussions with Nasser would have included questions of U.S. arms supply. Given the context that had developed and the intense feeling on those issues in Cairo and Jerusalem, settlement questions inevitably would have been subordinated, and the principal purpose of the mission, to see if there was a settlement alternative to major new arms supply, would likely have been lost in the shuffle.

Thirdly, as an independent but concerned American, nonofficial but with Washington support, I was in a position to establish my own relationship with Israeli and Egyptian leaders. Both sides knew I was in touch with the Department of State, but not needing to seek or follow instructions. Nasser, Sharett, and Ben-Gurion all responded warmly to that context. The leaders in both countries appeared to appreciate the opportunity to discuss in some depth the basic issues between them with someone whom they felt they could trust and who was not committed after each meeting to make an official report to Washington.

In sum, at that point in Middle Eastern developments I believe there were advantages in being a concerned but independent third party.

VI ～

Could the Outcome
Have Been Different?

IN ANY MAJOR settlement effort it is important in retrospect
to consider why it succeeded, why it failed, or why it met with only
partial success. Were there things that could have been done which
might have changed the outcome? Does the experience hold any
lessons for the future in dealing with the issues involved? In this
case, the answer to both questions is yes.

There was no doubt about the commitment of Dr. Fawzi and
Ambassador Hussein to the settlement effort. They had begun to
despair of Egypt getting any significant U.S. arms supply. They
foresaw the great difficulties that would ensue from an arms supply
agreement with the Soviet Union. An honorable political agreement, or at the minimum some acceptable modus vivendi with
Israel—difficult as it might be to achieve—seemed to them to be
the only effective way forward.

I had spent sufficient time alone in discussions with Prime Minister Nasser in August and early September to know that through
the first two rounds of talks he, too, was serious about the exploration. It is now clear that he had been a full party to Ambassador
Hussein's initiative in April and he had supported Dr. Fawzi's

strong endorsement in July.* He had cooperated actively in considering substantive issues and in helping defuse the escalating violence in the Gaza area late in August.

I had found Nasser direct, personally engaging, and disarming in his candor. I knew that others—in Israel and in the international community—believed him to be heady, impetuous, and often conspiratorial. There were times when these latter qualities were present to a complicating degree. But during the late spring and summer of 1955 he was prepared to respond seriously to the urging of Ambassador Hussein and Dr. Fawzi that settlement possibilities with Israel be thoroughly explored. The pathway he selected may have been due in part to his confidence—based on first-hand contact at Faluja in 1949—in the Quakers. But more importantly, while he did not share the deep convictions of his two colleagues about the potentially disastrous consequences of an arrangement for large-scale Eastern arms supply, it was clear from our discussions that he was sufficiently ill at ease with that prospect to join seriously in examining Israeli-Egyptian settlement possibilities.

Ben-Gurion was a shrewd judge of character and I do not believe he would have pressed so strongly for a face-to-face meeting with Nasser if he had thought the latter was conducting a charade to cloak his negotiations with the USSR.

Had we known at the time of the first meeting with Ambassador Hussein in April that his suggested exploration was strongly supported by Nasser, the negotiations would have gained very valuable time. But Ambassador Hussein, exercising caution, had suggested that he was giving his own opinion and not necessarily that of his government. From the beginning we took Hussein's initiative seriously, but it was from subsequent discussions with him and from the meeting with Dr. Fawzi in New York in July that we were able to conclude that Nasser fully supported the inquiry. Just how fully we would not know until my first meeting with Nasser in Cairo.

Nasser had been deeply embarrassed by the February Israeli attack on the Gaza Strip at a time when he considered that useful informal negotiations were under way. In the months after Ben-

*See page 29n.

Gurion took leave and Sharett became Prime Minister, he had developed considerable confidence in Sharett. The February attack came soon after Ben-Gurion returned to the cabinet as Defense Minister. Nasser blamed Ben-Gurion for the attack, but it raised doubts in his mind whether he could do business with either Sharett or Ben-Gurion. I had found Sharett moderate and farsighted and believe I had a hand in helping restore Nasser's confidence in him. Following the cancellation of the late August Israeli raid on Khan Yunis, and even after its reinstitution, Nasser for a time became intrigued with Ben-Gurion's suggestion that they should meet. He saw in Ben-Gurion a doughty character, a natural leader and an Israeli folk hero who could probably make a negotiated settlement stick. The suggestion of a meeting was thus not a preposterous idea. The recent Camp David experience illustrates the extent to which the basic issues in the Middle East can only be resolved at the highest level. The Israelis had indicated that once the negotiations got started Nasser would find them very flexible, and the discussions in Jerusalem had been such that I believed this would indeed be the case.

Nasser recognized it took decisiveness and some courage to cancel a raid—once launched—and his mind became less rigid on Ben-Gurion. Had the Israelis not reinstituted the raid two days later, Nasser's attitude toward Ben-Gurion would, I believe, have changed even further.

For a meeting between Nasser and Ben-Gurion to have taken place—even in these improved circumstances—would probably have required a major initial concessionary proposal from the Israeli leaders. It could have been a conditional proposal—dependent upon measures of reciprocity. But Sharett and Ben-Gurion were in a mood to consider just such a move. Ben-Gurion had become genuinely enthused over settlement possibilities; so much so that after I left Cairo for Washington, and only a few days before Nasser announced the Czech arms agreement, he stated that there were no real issues between Israel and Egypt.

Nasser would probably have insisted on some form of assurance on a cessation of Israeli military attacks against the Gaza Strip during any negotiations. In return the Israelis would have insisted that all fedayeen activity cease. Nasser knew that the latter would have been a requirement and he was prepared to make a major effort to control it. Because in any basic negotiation with Israel, Egypt would be vulnerable to political attacks from other Arab states, Israel would also have needed to cease all cross-border military activity while negotiations were under way. A situation had developed, however, in which these were no longer impossible considerations.

The Israeli leaders, of course, were aware of the possibilities of an Egyptian-Eastern European arms supply arrangement. They were not certain they could trust Nasser. They thought his shifting relationships with other Arab states made him an uncertain quantity. But over the summer they had been reassured by Nasser's actions and by early September, stirred by Ben-Gurion's enthusiasm, they were ready for major serious negotiations.

I have suggested that such negotiations and possibly a face-to-face meeting might have been possible if the Khan Yunis raid in late August had not been reinstituted—that that raid, laid on again following the cancellation two days earlier, had caused Nasser to say he needed time for things to cool down before resuming any negotiations on basic issues. Embarrassed by the timing of the February attack on the Gaza Strip, he concluded during my third visit to Cairo that the August Khan Yunis raid, even though initially canceled, continued an Israeli pattern of putting what he considered to be disproportionate retaliatory violence ahead of major efforts at settlement. He did not feel he could risk resuming basic negotiations without a period of time that attested to an Israeli policy change. Fortunately, sufficient confidence had been established and sufficient flexibility shown on basic issues by both sides by the time of the Khan Yunis attack for both to take action to defuse the situation—the Israelis by canceling the first attack orders, Nasser by canceling his mobilization broadcast.

Nasser was glad that the August violence had been brought under control, and he had been generous in his comments about the efforts I had made. But from our discussions I knew how unwilling he was to put himself in a position to be embarrassed again. Ben-Gurion and Nasser both had a flair for gaining and holding public attention. But Sadat's assassination many years later illustrates the risks run by any Arab leader who, in the highly charged atmosphere in the Middle East, moved publicly to seek peace with Israel.

There may be those who would maintain that sufficient progress had been made in the Egyptian-Czech arms talks by early September to preclude further meaningful Egyptian-Israeli negotiations. I do not believe, however, that by the time of my second visit to Cairo, beginning September 1, Nasser had made a final commitment for Eastern arms supply. Proposals had been developed and the Russians and Czechs had firmed up their offers, but Nasser could, I believe, have still at that time opted for a different course.* However, irrespective of the precise state of those negotiations during the first week in September, Nasser did not believe Eastern arms supply would prevent him from negotiating with the Israelis. He believed—taking a leaf from Nehru's diplomatic book—that such an arms supply agreement would strengthen his hand. He had no intention of becoming a Soviet satellite, and India's form of nonalignment was his objective. Only later did Nasser realize that Eastern European arms supply meant a large number of Soviet and Czech advisers and technicians. Ben-Gurion continued to talk about negotiations only days before the Czech agreement was announced. Nasser's belief that the arms accord would only strengthen his hand in negotiating with Israel was, following the Czech supply announcement, echoed by a number of diplomatic spokesmen who emphasized that a basic settlement with Israel was now more important and, perhaps, more possible than ever.†

In retrospect, it is clear I let the leaders on both sides weigh too long the possibilities of a face-to-face meeting, or some other form of direct negotiation. I should have realized that with the reinstituted Khan Yunis raid Nasser would retain sufficient doubts

---

*In his book *In Search of Identity* (pp. 127–28), Anwar el-Sadat refers to the Egyptian-Czech arms agreement as having been concluded in September.

†*New York Times,* October 6, 1955.

about Ben-Gurion to want a period of relative calm before he took on the political and personal risks of what in anyone's lexicon would have been a dramatic event. After talking with Nasser on the second visit to Cairo, a major effort should have been made to make the Eisenhower invitations operational. Whatever had been the agenda originally proposed for those discussions, by early September there was more than enough to discuss and it was time to call for maximum assistance. The call might not have been successful, but meetings arranged in early September—even if to be held later—might have made a difference.

With the negotiations with the United States on arms supply and on the Washington visit both appearing to Nasser to be stalemated, and a cooling off period needed, he believed, in Israeli-Egyptian relations, he was faced with a decision he had hoped to avoid.

Ben-Gurion, stirred deeply by the belief that a settlement could be achieved if only he and Nasser could get together, continued for another six months to talk hopefully about the possibility of a meeting. But there are times and seasons for everything, and often if opportunity is not seized, malleable political and personal contexts that could have been shaped to a larger and more significant purpose can quickly disappear. This is doubly the case when national leadership is young, revolutionary, and not deeply anchored in the patterns and traditions of the past.

Nasser's ultimate decision was a product of his continuing impasse with the United States, the initial attractiveness of the Eastern European offer, and his eventual assessment that his relations with the other Arab states would not sustain a meeting with Ben-Gurion without more assurance that cross-border violence would be brought under control.

So the settlement we sought had eluded our grasp. There were some pluses. The negotiations had clarified areas of flexibility on basic issues and had defused a situation late in August that appeared to be headed for major hostilities. They also had developed on both sides a greater understanding of the requirements and possibilities of negotiation. Subsequently the two governments were able to complete arrangements, agreed to in principle in early September, for a prisoner exchange.

There is both current and historical importance in Nasser having initiated the settlement exploration. President Sadat was not the first Egyptian leader to have made an effort to resolve the conflict with Israel.

VII ❦

The Downhill Slide to Suez

THE EGYPTIAN-CZECH arms supply agreement had brought the Soviets into the Middle East. Under Khrushchev, however, their policy was changing to one more supportive of nonalignment. The Egyptian arms agreement was a significant move forward in that new policy.

Over the preceding six months U.S. policy had drifted. Secretary Dulles had initially gotten some satisfaction from the development of the Baghdad Pact. But with vigorous opposition continuing from Israel and Egypt, with British unhappiness over the U.S. refusal to join, and with the U.S. feeling that the British were using the Pact to maintain their position in the area, British-American tension over the Middle East mounted.

Iraq had been the only Arab state to join the Pact and Syria, whom the U.S. had considered a potential adherent, was moving toward a closer relationship with Egypt. With Egypt destined to receive large supplies of arms from Eastern Europe, and with Israel concluding a major arms agreement with France, the Middle East presented a gloomy if not an alarming prospect.

During the spring and summer of 1955 Secretary Dulles and his Washington colleagues had been unprepared to accept the possibility that, in the absence of U.S. arms or a settlement with Israel, Nasser might turn to Eastern Europe for arms supply. The first reaction in Washington to the Czech arms agreement was thus one of major shock. The second reaction was of the need for damage limitation.

The first of the damage limitation moves reflected the unreality of U.S. Middle Eastern policy during the preceding months.

In July a Great Power Summit Meeting had been held in Geneva. The Foreign Ministers of the U.S., U.K., France, and the USSR were scheduled to hold a follow-up meeting in Geneva in October. The July meeting had exuded confidence about the future of East-West relations and this rosy aura infused the planning for the October meeting. It was thus not surprising that promptly following Nasser's announcement on September 27 the three Western powers emphasized to the Soviet Union that they considered the arrangement to supply arms to Egypt flew in the face of "the Geneva Spirit." None considered that the arms agreement could be undone, but there was hope that by vigorous representations to the Soviets, the three powers could head off Eastern European arms deals with other Arab states. The new agenda for Western discussions with Cairo was obviously to design a policy that took into account the fact that Egypt by June 1956, following the evacuation of British troops from Suez, would be in military control of the Suez Canal area and that she now considered herself as nonaligned. Designing such a policy was not something that could be done overnight.

Sharett and Dr. Fawzi both came to the fall session of the UN General Assembly, and during their periods in New York I met with each several times, continuing the review of basic issues. But it was not a time conducive to progress being made. Everyone was still trying to assess the meaning of the momentous events that had taken place at the end of September. Both men, however, carried back messages (Sharett to Ben-Gurion and Dr. Fawzi to Nasser) that kept the summer exploratory effort alive.

Soon after I returned to the U.S. I had reviewed the negotiations with Jacob Blaustein, and he had urged that I keep in close touch with the leaders on both sides—in case a further opening occurred.

Another person who was most helpful at this point was James Marshall, a close friend and a member of the New York law firm of Marshall, Bratter, Greene, Allison and Tucker. Jim and his family had long been active in the work of the Hebrew University in Jerusalem, and he had kept in close touch with general developments in the Middle East. He had been active in the work of the American Jewish Committee, and President of the New York City Board of Education. Together with his wife, Lenore, a talented poet, we spent many hours during the autumn considering ways in which political events might be directed toward a more promising prospect.

But much of the initiative was now in the hands of governmental actors as they attempted to fashion policies that took into account Egypt's new role.

Dag Hammarskjold, the United Nations Secretary-General, was one of those who took some needed initiative. A Swedish economist who was elected to the UN post because it was believed he would be a good administrator, he had turned out, to the surprise of many of his early sponsors, to be a brilliant and perceptive practitioner of quiet diplomacy. Through Andrew Cordier, his Executive Assistant, and Colonel Alfred Katzin, a South African who served as a Special Adviser, Hammarskjold had heard of the summer's exploration and, early in October, sent word that he would like to see me. But with characteristic efficiency, he said he would like to postpone our meeting until shortly before the General Assembly took up the Middle Eastern issues. The call from his office came, with customary precision, just two days before the first of the cluster of Middle Eastern issues arose in the Assembly. It was not the first time we had met, and when I arrived he gave instructions that we were not to be disturbed for anything less than a major crisis. We spent two hours reviewing the summer effort and discussing possible next steps.

Since becoming Secretary-General Hammarskjold had not visited the Middle East; nor was he acquainted with the Israeli and Egyptian leaders. He was looking forward to a visit to the area in connection with a 'round-the-world trip in January, following the General Assembly. He wanted in particular, and as a result of the

summer negotiations, to have my impressions of Ben-Gurion, Sharett, Nasser, and Dr. Fawzi. His questions were, as usual, penetrat-
ing and very relevant. How interested were the Israeli and Egyptian leaders in a resolution of the Arab-Israeli conflict? What had
I found to be the relationships between Ben-Gurion and Sharett?
What were Ben-Gurion's and Nasser's images of each other? What
kinds of risks of disruption of his relationships with other Arab
states was Nasser prepared to run to get a basic resolution of the
conflict with Israel?

I answered his questions as best I could. I emphasized that
Ben-Gurion was an able and effective leader of his people. To them
he was a patriarchal figure. He had deep religious and philosophical interests and enjoyed their pursuit. He could, however, make
tough decisions. Periodically his authorization of heavy military
raids across the armistice lines, in retaliation for cross-border terrorist activity—in what many observers considered to be disproportionate violence—got in the way of his otherwise steady vision
of what future cooperation between Jews and Arabs could mean
to the Middle East.

While Ben-Gurion was a patriarchal figure, Nasser, I suggested,
was to some extent his opposite. He was the young, determined,
and sometimes impetuous leader, with a deep sense of the needs of
the Egyptian people, and hoping to use that base to bring some
unity to the larger Arab community.

I explained to Hammarskjold the Egyptian origins of the summer settlement effort and we talked at some length about the
human equations which led to its initiation and which permitted
it to go forward. I felt that over the summer, levels of confidence
had been reached that went substantially below the surface with
both Ben-Gurion and Nasser and that had we had a little more
time definite progress might have been made. On the Egyptian side
Dr. Fawzi and Ambassador Hussein had been extraordinarily
helpful. I had come to have great respect for their skill and wisdom.
I had developed similar feelings about Prime Minister Sharett and
Gideon Rafael in Israel. It was not at all clear that Sharett could
carry the day over Ben-Gurion on any major substantive issue on
which they differed, but I suggested it was not too difficult, after

talking with both of them, to come to a conclusion as to what Israeli policy would be.

Hammarskjold's question about Nasser's and Ben-Gurion's images of each other was more difficult to answer. I believed that as a result of the negotiations, Ben-Gurion's conviction that he could do business with Nasser—if only they could get together—was clearly strengthened, and this conviction had survived the Egyptian-Czech arms agreement. But Ben-Gurion's basic assessment of Nasser continued to fluctuate between a belief that he was conspiratorial and could not be trusted, and the belief that the two of them could work out a settlement that could transform the Middle East. Nasser's picture of Ben-Gurion was not dissimilar. He felt that each time he initiated informal discussions with Israel, Ben-Gurion authorized some form of retaliatory military action that made it necessary for him to break off the meetings. At the same time he felt that Ben-Gurion was someone who could negotiate a settlement and make it stick.

I did not think Nasser had a clear idea of how much initiative he could take toward a settlement with Israel and still carry key Arab states with him.

Hammarskjold expressed appreciation for our frank discussion, which was to be continued early in January just before he left for the Middle East.

President Eisenhower's recuperation from his heart attack had gone well and he returned to Washington early in November. Sparked by the concern of Herbert Hoover, Jr., Secretary Dulles's Undersecretary, the U.S. by mid-December had put together a program through which it hoped to forestall further Soviet inroads into the Middle East. The United States announced it was prepared to join Britain and the World Bank in financing the construction of Egypt's largest project—the High Dam at Aswan. Soon after the Czech arms agreement Daniel Solod, the Soviet Ambassador in Cairo, had extended a Soviet offer to finance the dam. But Nasser, not wishing to open up another aspect of Egyptian life to Soviet influence, had made it clear he strongly preferred World Bank and Western assistance. And with the stakes having been substantially increased, Washington decided it was now feasible to override the domestic resistance of Israeli supporters and American cotton growers which had earlier been deterrents to the U.S.'s offering financial aid for High Dam construction.

There was to be a second major initiative in U.S. Middle Eastern policy. Washington decided to couple the Aswan Dam financing with a determined effort to get the peace process between Egypt and Israel moving again.

In January it sent Robert B. Anderson, a very successful Texas business leader and a close friend of the President, on an unpublicized mission to Cairo and Jerusalem. Anderson formerly had been Secretary of the Navy, then Deputy Secretary of Defense, and subsequently served as Secretary of the Treasury.

The proposals of Dulles's August speech constituted the basic agenda, and Anderson was instructed to offer, in addition to Aswan Dam financing, a U.S. guarantee of agreed borders and major economic aid to help Israel pay compensation to Palestine refugees.* It was a formidable assignment. But Anderson, an attractive and able man, had little experience with Middle Eastern questions. Traveling in military planes and avoiding contacts with the two U.S. embassies, he shuttled between Cairo and Jerusalem. But no progress was made. Ben-Gurion was still pressing for direct Israeli-Egyptian discussions—in particular between himself and Nasser—and was interested in talking with the U.S. only about arms. Nasser, increasingly aware of public opinion in Egypt and other Arab countries and upset over the Israeli attack on Kinnereth, Syria, in December—which left more than seventy Syrians dead—was now not prepared for any negotiations with Israel, even through third parties. He was willing to talk seriously about peace only if the U.S. could tell him in advance what the boundary adjustments would be.

At the end of February Mr. Anderson made a second unpublicized visit to the area, again shuttling between Jerusalem and Cairo. Again no progress was made. It was not a situation in which the earlier proposals of the U.S. for separate meetings in Washington between Eisenhower and Nasser, and Eisenhower and Ben-

---

*Neff, *Warriors at Suez,* p. 131.

Gurion or Sharett, would likely have borne fruit. The failure of the two Anderson missions underscored the difficulty of moving toward peace in the Middle East. But it also set the stage for Eisenhower's moving to more of an anti-Nasser stance.

History has a way of invalidating good ideas with the march of unanticipated events. Largely unrecognized, the downhill slide to the British-French-Israeli attack on Suez in November 1956 was now under way.

Meanwhile Hammarskjold in January had made his first trip to the Middle East, on the first leg of his 'round-the-world trip. I saw him shortly before he left and we updated impressions of developments in the area. His primary substantive concern was the encroachments of the Israelis and the Egyptians on the El Auja demilitarized zone lying between Israeli and Egyptian forces in the Sinai. But he was equally interested in the opportunity the trip gave him to become acquainted with government leaders—including in Israel and Egypt.

This first trip produced very limited results, and as violence grew across the armistice lines, the UN Security Council on April 4 asked Hammarskjold to proceed immediately to the Middle East on a second trip to develop and seek agreement on measures that would reduce tensions along the armistice demarcation lines. The violence was a product not only of local incidents but also of the deteriorating political context now surrounding Middle East affairs. Thus the assignment was an extraordinarily difficult one and the impressions and friendships formed on his January trip proved very important. Ben-Gurion soon found that Hammarskjold was a tough and well-informed negotiator. It was not long before they found that they enjoyed broad philosophical discussion.* It became a close relationship that often was subjected to the strain of retaliatory violence, but it proved to be a touchstone helping to resolve many issues that otherwise might have proved more than the traffic could bear. Hammarskjold was not so impressed with Sharett. The Secretary-General and Nasser did not in

*Brian Urquhart, *Hammarskjold* (New York: Alfred A. Knopf, 1972); see pages 151–52.

the beginning take to each other, but they soon found a relationship based on mutual respect. Hammarskjold was much impressed with Dr. Fawzi's wisdom and skill, although he recognized the limitations in his influence. They were to become fast friends.

In his four weeks of negotiation Hammarskjold succeeded in getting new commitments from Israel and her four Arab neighbors to adhere fully to the Armistice Agreements. It was hailed as a remarkable achievement, and in view of the difficulties and the deteriorating political context in the Middle East, it was. Hammarskjold had suggested in our meeting early in January that he was prepared informally to explore new avenues to a more substantial easing of tensions in the area. But after becoming more deeply involved he decided that he would not seek such a role but respond only if others suggested it.

While a larger role for the Secretary-General did not develop at this stage, the April achievement helped set the stage for substantial United Nations involvement in early November when the British, French, and Israeli forces made their dramatic attack on Suez.

It was not long after the announcement on December 16, 1955, that the U.S., Britain and the World Bank would join in financing the Aswan Dam that the U.S. began to have second thoughts. Eisenhower became unhappy as the Anderson mission made no progress and domestic opposition mounted to the Aswan financing. It was an election year and Democratic leaders were urging that the tight U.S. limitations on arms to the area be relaxed with substantial arms being provided to Israel.

In the meantime French and British relations with Cairo were deteriorating. The French were convinced, mistakenly, that Nasser, in addition to his diplomatic support of the rebel Front de Libération Nationale (FLN) in Algeria, was providing large-scale military and economic assistance. The conviction caused France to accelerate her diplomatic support and arms supply to Israel.

British relations with Cairo were becoming no less strained. At the time of Iraqi independence in 1932 Britain had retained certain treaty rights. It is thus not so surprising that Iraq should have been drawn into the Baghdad Pact. Britain had also hoped to draw Jordan, where she also had retained rights, into the Pact. But in a series of moves highly embarrassing to the British, involving the dismissal by King Hussein of Sir John Bagot Glubb (Glubb Pasha) from his position as Commander of the Arab Legion and his expulsion from the country, Hussein, supported by Nasser, was able to thwart the British plans. Prime Minister Eden had already taken a decided dislike to Nasser, but his disappointment over the developments in Jordan fixed his suspicions and resentment on what became an irreversible course. The Israelis had made their own contribution to the inflamed atmosphere in Jordan with the large-scale attack on Kinnereth, Syria.

Encouraged by Israeli and Egyptian officials I again made a trip to the Middle East in April, while Hammarskjold was on his armistice supporting negotiation. Ben-Gurion, now the Israeli Prime Minister, was still pondering over why the effort the previous summer had not succeeded. He was certain a major breakthrough could have taken place if only he and Nasser could have gotten together. He was not now prepared to offer any concessions, but he again outlined, with eloquence and fervor, what he considered to be the many advantages of a peace between Israel and her Arab neighbors.

This time in Cairo, Nasser invited me to his home. He said Egyptian-U.S. relations had improved somewhat during the preceding months. But an early trip to the U.S. no longer seemed a likely possibility. He opened up a discussion on Ben-Gurion, saying he could not figure out what he was after. Ben-Gurion, he said, seemed to want peace with the Arabs but he also "seemed to think of them as they were fifty years ago." He thought Ben-Gurion's return to the Israeli cabinet and the Baghdad Pact were the two recent catastrophes in the area. All sorts of difficulties, he said, had stemmed from these events. My suggestion that I believed Ben-Gurion was genuinely interested in and very likely in an excellent position to negotiate a settlement did not bring an encouraging response. He emphasized, however, that his door would always be open and that he would be glad to see me at any time. Like Ben-Gurion he was not prepared to consider any concessions.

While Washington now shared much of the British and French uneasiness about Nasser, it did not like their strident tone. On June

19 the British completed their evacuation of the Suez Canal base. Three days later, following a plebiscite and a wave of public acclaim, Nasser was elected President of Egypt.

But things were now not going well on Aswan Dam financing. The foot-dragging in Washington had continued and when Eugene Black, President of the World Bank, announced in late June that the Bank was prepared to move forward, there was no response from the U.S. Then on July 19 Dulles informed Ambassador Ahmed Hussein that the United States was withdrawing its offer to help finance the Aswan project. Britain promptly followed suit. With its two partners out, it was no longer feasible for the World Bank to continue.

It was a body blow that Nasser felt left him only one alternative. The Suez Canal company was an Egyptian company, and after a quick analysis of the legalities, Nasser on July 26 announced in Alexandria that Egypt was taking over the company. It was the fourth anniversary of King Farouk's abdication. The action set in motion the forces that were to culminate, November 6, in the British-French-Israeli attack on Suez in an effort to recover the canal—a military operation that set the Middle East aflame and threatened a wider confrontation.

President Eisenhower, unable to perform what might have been a decisive preventive role a year earlier, vigorously condemned the attack and, in company with the USSR, insisted on a complete withdrawal of the British, French, and Israeli forces. U.S. standing in Egypt rose dramatically, but Israeli-Egyptian settlement possibilities suffered a major setback.

Epilogue

DURING THE INTENSE negotiations preceding the Egyptian-Czech arms accord I had come to be very fond of both Ben-Gurion and Nasser. From the beginning I felt Sharett understood his Arab adversaries. But Ben-Gurion and Nasser were the principals in the situation and it was essential that they reach some understanding. I had been able to interpret each to the other in ways that appeared to increase the interest of both in finding a solution. I had worked hard to do my homework on the basic issues. But most of my discussions with the three men had also included questions of philosophical and ethical beliefs. I wanted to know what kind of persons I was dealing with—so I would know something about their convictions, what they felt was important, and how they would be likely to respond when the going got tough. Fortunately both Ben-Gurion and Nasser had religious interests and, through their experience with Quaker humanitarian work, both had developed sufficient curiosity about Quaker beliefs to be interested in discussing such questions.

In the process Ben-Gurion and Nasser became intensely interested in the other's beliefs, and I spent some time interpreting to Nasser Ben-Gurion's experience with U Nu and explaining to

Ben-Gurion the experiences that lay behind Nasser's book *Egypt's Liberation: The Philosophy of the Revolution.* We always came back to the political issues, but these interludes had provided many of the insights that made it possible to build confidence and create the interest which made a face-to-face meeting between Israeli and Egyptian leaders a subject of serious consideration.* I was reminded of George Taylor of the Wharton School of the University of Pennsylvania, one of America's most successful labor mediators, who once advised, "When the going gets tough, change the pace." I do not know how summaries of these philosophical discussions would have looked in State Department cables, but the discussions themselves proved to be an important dimension in the summer effort.

The discussion of these deeply held religious and philosophical questions continued to be intermingled with consideration of political issues well into the following year. Perhaps this should not be all that surprising. It was the Middle East that gave birth to three of the world's great religions. And over the years many of the noblest efforts and the most atrocious deeds have been carried out in their name.

There is something about the Middle East that, once one has been exposed, gets an enduring grip on one's emotions: Beirut, now tortured but still nestled dramatically between the Mediterranean Sea and the snow-capped Lebanon range; Baalbek and the broad Bekaa valley; Damascus and its eternal springs; Jerusalem with its luminous stone foundations and its panoramic view; the red sandstone desert setting of Petra; and Cairo, with its museums and its pyramids attesting to the area's long rendezvous with history. And against this scenic and noble background are the people—varied,

---

*Years later, after Ben-Gurion had retired a second time and while he was writing his memoirs, one of his former assistants, Jacob Hertzog, accompanied Prime Minister Golda Meir on a trip to New York. Hertzog called me to say that before leaving Jerusalem Ben-Gurion had telephoned him from the Negev to ask him to ask me if I thought Nasser was interested in a meeting with him because of his position with the Israeli government or because he saw in him an able and effective leader of the Israeli people. I replied that I was certain both factors were important considerations for Nasser.

colorful, rich and poor, attached to their land, made uncertain by the impact of modernization and the clash of cultures, but most of all, long-suffering—very, very long-suffering. It is an area over which quantities of blood have been shed. Must it always be so?

The history of efforts to resolve regional issues in the Middle East is replete with failures and near-misses. The Armistice Agreements, achieved by the UN's Ralph Bunche, and the Camp David accords are notable exceptions. In a situation of prolonged hostility it is difficult to place confidence in untested measures whose effectiveness is unknown. The drama of Sadat's trip to Jerusalem and the overwhelmingly favorable response of the Egyptian and Israeli people made it possible for both governments to think in terms of substituting political for military security. Sadat's assassination illustrates the risks inherent in attempting to demonstrate the viability of that alternative. In most conflict situations there are groups whose interests lie in preventing a settlement.

In the summer of 1955, in the months before the Egyptian-Czech arms agreement, Ben-Gurion became excited over the possibilities of a peace settlement. Nasser also had a positive picture in his mind of what a settlement would mean for Egypt and the Middle East. But both men in the end allowed certain things, comparatively minor in the sweep of history, to get in the way. For Ben-Gurion it was his willingness to support one more major retaliatory foray. For Nasser it was his felt need for a period of calm that would attest to the ending of what he considered to be Israel's policy of disproportionate military retaliation.

In 1971 Flora Lewis of the *New York Times* asked Mr. Ben-Gurion for his thoughts in retrospect about the effectiveness of terrorist violence. Subsequently the then sage elder statesman sent her a handwritten note that said, "I will limit my answer to your question on terror only to Israel. The acts of terror in Eretz Israel were unjust, useless, and shameful."* Had Nasser still been living it would have been of immense interest to have gotten his response to Ben-Gurion's reflection.

Nasser and Sadat have not been the only Arab leaders to explore

---

*New York Times, August 7, 1981.

the bases on which hostilities in the Middle East could be brought
to an end. Others have tried. King Hussein of Jordan has in the
past been heavily criticized by Arab colleagues for several efforts
to find the basis for an honorable settlement.

But President Nasser had a unique position in the Arab world.
He was a symbol of Arab nationalism, and the Egyptian revolution
had stirred deep emotions throughout the Arab world. The fact
that Nasser explored seriously the possibilities of a peace settlement with Israel—before he turned to Eastern Europe for arms
supply—should be of major interest to all those who seek an end
to the cycles of violence that periodically convulse the Middle East.

Chronology

1947

November 29   United Nations adopts Palestine partition resolution.

1948

May 14   Termination of the British Mandate over
(midnight)   Palestine.

May 15   Proclamation of the State of Israel.

            United States announces de facto recognition of
            Israel.

            Secretary-General of the Arab League informs
            Secretary-General of the United Nations that the
            Arab states had decided to take up arms against
            Israel.

            Soviet Union grants de jure recognition to Israel.

September 17 Assassination of Count Folke Bernadotte, United
            Nations Mediator, by Jewish assailants in
            Jerusalem.

November 16   UN Security Council calls for Armistice
            Agreements, to be negotiated by Dr. Ralph

Bunche, Acting UN Mediator, terminating
hostilities between Israel and Egypt, Jordan,
Syria, and Lebanon.

December 11 UN General Assembly, meeting in Paris, adopts a
general resolution calling for a termination of the
Palestine conflict by direct negotiations or with
the assistance of an especially appointed UN
Conciliation Commission, and for the solution of
the refugee problem by repatriation of those
willing to live at peace with their neighbors and
compensation of those who prefer not to return.

1949
February Israeli-Egyptian Armistice negotiated by Ralph
Bunche, Acting UN Mediator (Armistice
Agreements followed between Israel and Jordan,
Syria and Lebanon).

May 11 The United Nations accepts Israel into
membership.

1950
May 25 Britain, France, and the United States adopt
Tripartite Declaration, with the objective of
rationing arms sales to countries involved in the
Arab-Israeli conflict.

1951
October 15 The Wafd government in Egypt denounces the
1936 Treaty with Britain on Suez. Britain
responds with an arms embargo.

1952
July 23 The Free Officers Group, led by Colonel Nasser,
topples the Farouk Government in a largely
bloodless coup. Nasser was promptly elected as
chairman of the Revolutionary Command
Council. Subsequently, because of his seniority
and at Nasser's request, Major General
Mohammed Naguib was elected chairman of the
Council.

July 26 King Farouk abdicates and leaves the country.

1953

April 17   British open talks with the new revolutionary
government in Egypt on evacuation of British
forces from the Suez Canal base.

October 12   Israeli raid on Qibya in Jordan; sixty-six villagers
killed, seventy-five others suffer wounds and
severe injuries, forty-five homes are blown up.

December 7   After several months' leave, Ben-Gurion resigns
as Prime Minister and retires to Sde Boker
kibbutz in the Negev. Moshe Sharett, who had
been deputizing for Ben-Gurion, becomes Prime
Minister, retaining the Foreign Ministership.

1954

March   Nasser becomes Prime Minister of Egypt.

July 9   Eleven alleged Israeli spies, operating under the
apparent direction of Israeli military intelligence,
and without Prime Minister Sharett's knowledge,
attempt to sabotage U.S. and British installations
in Cairo and Alexandria.

July 27   Britain and Egypt initial an accord defining terms
for British withdrawal from Suez.

October 19   Britain and Egypt sign final accord providing for
British withdrawal from Suez within twenty
months, bringing to an end Britain's seventy-five
year occupation of Egyptian territory.

November   A representative of the Moslem Brotherhood
attempts to assassinate Nasser, believing that the
Suez Canal accord gave the British too long to
withdraw.

November 14   General Mohammed Naguib resigns as President
of Egypt and goes into permanent retirement.

November   Eisenhower offers Egypt $27 million in military
aid and $13 million in economic aid.

December 11   Trials of eleven alleged Israeli spies begin in
Cairo—running to January 5, 1955.

1955

February 17   Ben-Gurion returns to the Israeli cabinet as Defense Minister.

February 28   Israel launches a heavy raid on Gaza. The Egyptian forces suffered eighty-five casualties, with forty soldiers killed. Eight Israeli soldiers were killed and nine wounded.

July-September   *Egyptian-Israeli negotiations in an attempt to get a settlement or a modus vivendi as an alternative to an Egyptian-Eastern European arms supply agreement.*

September 27   Nasser announces Egyptian-Czech arms supply accord.

November 2   Ben-Gurion resumes Prime Ministership in Israel.

1956

January–February   Robert B. Anderson, personal representative of President Eisenhower, makes two trips to the Middle East in an attempt to establish the basis for an Arab-Israeli settlement. No progress is made.

January   Dag Hammarskjold, UN Secretary-General, visits the Middle East as part of his first world tour.

April 6   Hammarskjold leaves for four-week trip to the Middle East to explore, and if possible to arrange for, measures for reinforcing the Armistice Agreements.

June 19   British complete the evacuation of their forces on the Suez Canal.

June 22   Nasser is elected President of Egypt, following a plebiscite. The Revolutionary Council is dissolved.

July 26   The Egyptian government nationalizes the Suez Canal.

November 6   Britain, France, and Israel launch an attack on Suez in an attempt to regain the canal.

APPENDIX I

"The Quakers"

Address by Gunnar Jahn, Chairman, Nobel Committee, and
Director of the Bank of Norway, at the presentation of The
Nobel Peace Prize, Oslo, December 10, 1947

IT IS NOW three hundred years since George Fox laid the
foundation of the community of Quakers. It was during a time of
civil war in England, a period filled with religious and political
strife which led to the Protectorate under Cromwell. Today we
would probably call it a dictatorship. The same thing happened
then as on so many other occasions when a political or religious
movement has been successful. It is apt to forget what it originally
set out to achieve, namely its right to freedom. When the movement has come into power it will not grant to others what
it struggled to obtain for itself. That is what happened in the case
of the Presbyterians and in the case of the Independents after
them. It was not the spirit of toleration and humanity that con-
quered.

This was experienced by George Fox and many of his associates
during the ensuing years, but they did not take up an armed fight
such as the custom is among men. They went their own quiet way
because they were opposed to any use of force. They believed that

in the long run spiritual weapons would lead to victory, and this belief had been acquired through inward experience. What they regarded as important was life itself and not the forms it assumed. Formalities, theories and doctrines have never been a matter of importance to them, and, therefore, from the outset, they have been a community without any strict organization. This has given the movement an inner strength, a more unbiased view of their fellow men, and a greater degree of toleration towards others than is found in most organized religious communities.

In the beginning the Quaker movement was limited to England, but at an early stage, in 1656, they found their way to the United States of America where, at first, they were not welcome. But they held out in spite of persecution, and in the last quarter of the century they gained a firm foothold. Everybody has heard about William Penn, the Quaker who founded Philadelphia and the colony of Pennsylvania. It is believed that as early as about 1700 there were 50–60,000 Quakers in the United States and about the same number in England.

Since that time the Quakers have led their own lives. Many of them have had to suffer for their faith, and many things have changed during these three hundred years. Outward customs in respect to clothing, adopted by the first Quakers, have been discarded. The Quakers now live in a community which externally is entirely different from the community of the seventeenth century; but the people around them have not changed, and the obstacles to be surmounted within the individual men and women have not diminished.

The community of Quakers had never been numerous, hardly very much more than well over 200,000 in the whole world. The majority live in the United States and England. However, it is not the number that matters. What counts is their inner strength and their deeds.

If we study the history of the Quakers we are overwhelmed by the fortitude which they have acquired, through their faith and by trying to live up to that faith. They have always been opposed to the use of force in any form or shape. The fact that they have refused to take part in war has led many people to believe that this is the essential part of their religion. But the matter is not quite so simple. It is true that the declaration of 1660 contains the following words: "We utterly deny all outward wars and strife and fighting with outward weapons to any end and under any pretense whatever. This is our testimony to the whole world." In this declaration there is implied much more than a mere refusal to take part in war. It amounts to the following: It is better to suffer injustice than to exercise injustice. In the end victory must come from within the individual man or woman.

Presumably it is safe to say, without doing injustice to anyone, that during certain periods the Quakers have directed more attention to themselves and their inward lives than to the society in which they were living. As one of their own historians has said, there was an element of passivity in their attitude. They wanted to be regarded as belonging to those who are the quiet in the land. But no person can fulfill his work in life if he will only be one of the quiet and live his own life isolated from others.

Nor was this course of action adopted by the Quakers. They, too, were to go out among the people, not in order to convert them, but in order to participate actively in community life and, still more, in order to offer their aid where aid was needed, and in order to let good deeds make their own appeal and so to establish contact between men.

On this occasion I can only mention some casual features to throw light on what the Quakers have done. They took part in the creation of the first peace organization in 1810, and since then they have assisted in all active peace movements. I would mention Elizabeth Fry, John Woolman, and their associates in their campaign against slavery and their struggle for social justice. I would also refer to that liberal idealist, John Bright, and his forty years of struggle against the principles of war and for the principles of peace, his opposition to the Crimean War and his fight against Palmerston's policy. Many other examples might be mentioned of how their active efforts in community work—or in politics, if you prefer that word—increased during the nineteenth century.

But it is not this aspect of their activities—the positive, political aspect—which places the Quakers in a special position. It is the silent help from the nameless to the nameless which is their contribution to the promotion of brotherhood among nations, as it is expressed in the will of Alfred Nobel. Their work started in the prisons. During the Napoleonic War we heard about them from our seamen who "were in prison years on end," and we heard about them again during the Irish famine in 1846–47. When British naval forces had bombarded the Finnish coast during the Crimean War, the Quakers went there to heal the wounds of war. They were also in France when war had ravaged in that country in 1870–71.

When the First World War broke out, the Quakers again experienced what it meant to suffer for their faith. They refused to carry arms, and many of them were put into prison, where they were often worse treated than if they had been criminals. But it is not these events which will remain longest in our memory. We who have lived consciously through the First World War and the interwar period will probably most clearly remember the reports of their work to relieve the distress caused by the war. As early as 1914 the English Quakers started to prepare relief schemes. They set to work in the Marne district of France, and to the largest practicable extent they were on the spot where there had been devastations of war. In this manner they went on during the whole war. When it was over, they had to face even greater tasks. Then —as now—hunger and sickness followed in the wake of war. We all remember the years of famine in Russia in 1920–21 and Nansen's appeal to humanity for aid. We remember the misery of the children in Vienna which lasted year after year. Everywhere the Quakers took part in the work. The Friends Service Committee undertook, at Mr. Hoover's request, the enormous task of providing food to the sick and undernourished children in Germany. Their assistance corps was in activity in Poland and Serbia, and they continued their work in France. Later on, during the civil war in Spain, they rendered help on both sides of the front.

The Quakers gained confidence in all quarters through their work. Governments and individuals knew that they had no other aim than to aid. They did not intrude on people in order to convert them to their faith, and they made no difference between friend and foe. It is proof of this confidence that the Quakers were put in charge of large funds which had been given by others. The means which the Quakers themselves could afford would not have amounted to very much, as most Quakers are people of small means.

During the interwar period the scope of their social service activities was also extended. In a certain sense it was not a new development, but it was rather a change in the character of the problems which led to another form of activities. Constructive work became more important, education and teaching played a greater part, and there was more opportunity for talking to people than during a time when the one and only necessity seemed to be to provide food and clothes. What the Quakers achieved among American miners in West Virginia is an impressive example of their activities. They have solved the housing problem and provided new work for the unemployed. They have created a little new community. As one of their own members has written, they have succeeded in restoring self-respect and confidence in life in people to whom living seemed hopeless. And that is only one example out of many.

The Second World War did not affect the Quakers personally in the same manner as the war of 1914. Both in England and the United States the conscription laws allowed the Quakers to perform other duties instead of military service, so they were not put in prison or persecuted because they would not take part in war. Incidentally, during this war some Quakers did not refuse to take an active part in the fighting; but their number was small compared to those who chose to take up work in aid of the victims of war. When the war broke out the first task that awaited them was to help the refugees. But great difficulties were encountered, as foreign frontiers were soon closed. The greater part of Europe was soon occupied by the Germans and the United States only remained neutral for a short time. In most places where the Germans came the Quakers were not admitted. It is true that in Poland they were allowed to help, but the Germans prescribed as a condition that they themselves should decide who was to receive aid, and on such terms the Quakers were unable to operate. Still, they worked where they could. First, they were connected with welfare work in England and, later on, behind the front in many countries of Europe, Asia, and also America, where the whole Japanese-American population—a total of 112,000 persons, of which 80,000 were American citizens—were evacuated from the West Coast. In this situation the Quakers came to their assistance and opposed the anti-Japanese feeling which was also causing injury to these people.

Since the war there has been more need for help than ever before. This not only applies to Europe but equally to large parts of Asia. The problems are gradually becoming overwhelming: Prisoners coming out of the concentration camps in 1945; all the people who had to be repatriated from compulsory labour or internment as prisoners of war in enemy countries; all the displaced persons who have no country to which they can return; all those who are homeless in their own country; all the orphans, all those who are starving or about to die from starvation. Here, it is not only a question of giving people food and clothes. It is a question of bringing them back to life and employment, of restoring their faith and confidence in the future ahead of them. It is a question of restoring the integrity of the individual. This time, also, the Quakers are taking part everywhere. As soon as a country was opened again, they were on the spot, in Europe as well as in Asia, among fellow countrymen and friends as well as among previous enemies, in France as well as in Germany, in India as well as in Japan. It is not easy to measure the extent of their aid, and it is not something which can be assessed in money. Still, perhaps it may be some indication that the budget of the American Committee for last year amounted to 46 million Norwegian kroner. And that figure shows only what the American Committee had at its disposal. Quakers from all countries have also taken an active and personal part in the work of other relief organizations. Thus they have taken part in the activities of UNRRA in several places, such as Vienna and Greece.

Today the Quakers are deeply engaged in an effort which will continue for many years to come. But even if we were to take a closer look at the individual relief schemes it would not give us any better insight into the real significance of their work. It is not the extent of their work or its practical form which is most important in assessing the services rendered by the Quakers to people whom they have met. It is rather the spirit which animates their work. "We weren't sent out to make converts," said a young Quaker, "we've come out for a definite purpose, to build up in a spirit of love what has been destroyed in a spirit of hatred. We're not missionaries. We can't tell if even one person will be converted to Quakerism. Things like that don't happen in a hurry. When our work is finished it doesn't mean that our influence died with it. We have not come out to show the world how wonderful we are. No, the thing that seems most important is the fact that while the world is waging a war in the name of Christ, we can bind up the wounds of war in the name of Christ. Religion means very little until it is translated into positive action."

This is the message of good deeds, the message that men can come into contact with one another in spite of war and in spite of difference of race. May we believe that here there is hope of laying a foundation for peace among nations, of building up peace in man himself, so that it becomes impossible to settle disputes by use of force. We all know that we have not advanced far along that way. And yet, when we now regard the great willingness to help those who have suffered, a generosity which was unknown before the war, and which is often greatest among those whose means are smallest, is there not still a hope that there is something in man's soul on which one can build, so that we shall succeed some day, if we are only given a chance to speak with people in all countries.

The Quakers have shown us that it is possible to carry into action something which is deeply rooted in the minds of many: Sympathy with others; that significant expression of sympathy between men, without regard to nationality or race; feelings which, when carried into deeds, must provide the foundations of a lasting peace. For this reason they are today worthy of receiving Nobel's Peace Prize.

But they have also given us something else: They have demonstrated the strength which is founded on the faith in the victory of spirit over force.

That recalls to my mind some lines in one of Arnulf Øverland's poems which helped so many of us during the war. I can give you no better message from us than these lines:

> The unarmed only
> has inexhaustible sources.
> Only the spirit can win.

APPENDIX II

Draft of a Letter

From Moshe Sharett, Prime Minister of Israel, to Gamal
Abdel Nasser, Prime Minister of Egypt, August 31, 1955

[THIS LETTER, DETAILING depredations into Israel from the
Gaza Strip just previous to the February 28, 1955, retaliatory raid
by Israel on Egyptian forces in Gaza—a raid that caused Nasser
to break off informal discussions with Israel—was written by
Sharett to be hand-carried to Nasser by Elmore Jackson on September 1, the day following the resumed Israeli raid on Khan
Yunis. Sharett initially thought that such a letter, explaining the
February circumstances, might prevent an escalation of violence
and help keep the negotiations going following the Khan Yunis
attack. But he finally decided, rather than sending the letter,
that it would be better to let Mr. Jackson handle the crisis in
his own way.]

I AM GLAD to have the opportunity to renew my personal
contact with you after an interval of several months during which
so many regrettable things have occurred.

Our desire for peace and cooperation with Egypt is sincere as
ever but we have been dismayed to see no signs of such a desire on

her part. Moreover, in the absence of formal peace it would seem vital that both parties should scrupulously observe the Armistice Agreement, yet what we are confronted with is constant violations of the armistice, growing in seriousness, by the armed forces of the Gaza Strip.

We know how deeply you were hurt by certain action on our part, but, judging by what we have heard, you do not seem to be aware that what happened on February 28 was the consequence of a series of organized armed incursions from the Gaza Strip into our territory, resulting in sabotage and murder and rendering life unsafe in a large area. These incidents may seem minor to an outsider. To us they are a most serious matter, completely destructive of security and creating a situation which is quite intolerable.

I am sure that as a soldier and patriot you would never tolerate a situation in which Egypt would have to abide by the terms of an armistice which the other side felt free to disregard.

You seem to be convinced that what occurred on Monday. . .* was an unprovoked attack by an Israel patrol on an Egyptian outpost, motivated by our desire to force your hands in the Gaza talks. I want to assure you that nothing is further from the truth and I am very deeply concerned to find that you should be misinformed to such an extent. It was your outpost which started firing while our patrol acted in self-defense. The decision to silence the outpost by attacking it was taken by the local commander and had no political purpose whatsoever. Far from trying to force your hands in the matter of the Gaza talks, we were eagerly waiting at the time for the return of General Burns from Cairo in order to see whether as a result of his intervention the gap between our respective attitudes has been narrowed.

Your decision to break off the talks was to us most disappointing. It left prey to anarchy a potentially dangerous situation which we had hoped the agreed results of the talks would bring under firm control.

*The date omissions in the text of the Prime Minister's letter were to be filled in by his aides, this first reference presumably being to Monday, February 28, and the second being to Thursday, February 24.

Our apprehensions were very quickly realised. On the night of Thursday . . . your troops at Gaza went into offensive action. They crossed the line at four points, ambushing and killing a settler traveling in a jeep, blowing up a well and occupying strongpoints within our territory from which they had to be ejected the following morning. On Friday and Saturday things were relatively quiet; we did not react to the events of Thursday night hoping that there would be no further trouble. But on Saturday night there was another spate of attacks from the Gaza Strip which resulted in further bloody ambushes and acts of sabotage. In addition, landmines which must have been laid by your people during that night caused on the following day the death of four of our soldiers including an officer. On the other hand, an exchange of fire which occurred on Sunday resulted, as we understand, in a number of casualties among your troops. On Monday morning Egyptian jet planes appeared over our territory and had to be driven back.

We deeply deplore this new tide of violence. Our impression of your statesmanship and earnest devotion to the cause of your people makes it impossible for us to assume that you should be indifferent to the pernicious results to which this dangerous process is bound to lead if it continues unchecked. We are driven to the conclusion that you are simply unaware of the gravity of the issue. On the other hand we are convinced that once you would appreciate the perils with which this situation is fraught and would send down to Gaza somebody with full authority on your part to take the situation very firmly in hand, complete quiet would be restored and no question of any retaliation on our part would ever arise.

It is up to you to cut the vicious circle by preventing your people from opening fire in an unprovoked manner, from mining our roads and from crossing the lines to perpetrate murder and destruction. On our part we shall fully cooperate. This is the call we address to you, for the sake of peace and for the good of our countries.

Of course, if a meeting between two responsible men were possible at this stage, many misunderstandings and disagreements from which both our countries are suffering might be eliminated.

Index